The Islamic Polity and Political Leadership

The Islamic Polity and Political Leadership

Fundamentalism, Sectarianism, and Pragmatism

Mehran Tamadonfar

Westview Press
BOULDER, SAN FRANCISCO, & LONDON

Westview Special Studies on the Middle East

This Westview softcover edition is printed on acid-free paper and bound in softcovers that carry the highest rating of the National Association of State Textbook Administrators, in consultation with the Association of American Publishers and the Book Manufacturer's Institute.

All rights reserved. No part of this publication may be reproduced or transmitted in any form or by any means, electronic or mechanical, including photocopy, recording, or any information storage and retrieval system, without permission in writing from the publisher.

Copyright © 1989 by Westview Press, Inc.

Published in 1989 in the United States of America by Westview Press, Inc., 5500 Central Avenue, Boulder, Colorado 80301, and in the United Kingdom by Westview Press, Inc., 13 Brunswick Centre, London WC1N 1AF, England

Library of Congress Cataloging-in-Publication Data
Tamadonfar, Mehran.
  The Islamic polity and political leadership.
  (Westview special studies on the Middle East)
  Bibliography: p.
  Includes index.
  1. Islam and State. I. Title. II. Series.
JC49.T35 1989   297'.1977   87-10647
ISBN 0-8133-7436-7

Printed and bound in the United States of America

∞   The paper used in this publication meets the requirements of the American National Standard for Permanence of Paper for Printed Library Materials Z39.48-1984.

10   9   8   7   6   5   4   3   2   1

To Diane, Emily and my parents

Contents

Acknowledgments	ix
Introduction	1

1   A Framework for Analysis   5

   The Study of Leadership: Significance and Status, 5

   Toward a Conceptual, Methodological and Theoretical Framework, 6
      Conceptualization, 6
      Methodology, 8
      Theoretical Models: A Synthesis, 10

   Selected Western Theoretical Frameworks for the Study of Islamic Political Leadership, 12
      Elite Theories, 12
      Theories of Charismatic Authority, 24

   Elitism, Charismatic Authority and Islamic Leadership, 28

   Notes, 30

2   The Islamic Polity   35

   Islam and Politics, 35

   The Islamic State, 38
      Foundations, 38
      An Alternative State, 40
      Characteristics, 44

   Notes, 56

3   The Politics of Islamic Sectarianism   61

   Monolithicism and Sectarianism, 61

Islamic Sectarianism: Foundations, Developments and Implications, 65

Notes, 72

4 Islamic Political Leadership: Fundamentalism, Sectarianism and Pragmatism   75

The Indispensability of Leadership, 76

Sectarianism and Political Leadership, 77
    The Sunni Doctrine of Khalifah, 78
    Doctrines of Imamah, 92
    Contemporary Leadership Doctrines, 103

Pragmatism in Political Leadership, 112
    The Khalifah *System*, 112
    The Imamah *System*, 115
    *Post-*Imamah *Leadership*, 118

Notes, 120

Conclusion   127

Glossary	133
Bibliography	137
Index	147

Acknowledgments

I am indebted to a number of people for their suggestions and advice during the preparation of this book. Foremost among them is my mentor and friend Professor William Safran who followed the development of this book from its conception to its conclusion. His questions led me to probe deeper; his suggestions invariably improved the manuscript; and his own work and innovative thinking served as an example worthy of emulation. I am also indebted to Professor Richard Pfaff of the University of Colorado and my colleagues and students at the University of Nevada–Las Vegas for their encouragement and patience.

My deepest appreciation goes to Ms. Barbara Ellington and her colleagues at Westview Press for their trust and guidance. Their suggestions for improving the manuscript were invaluable. I am also grateful to Kathleen Martin for her editorial contributions. Last, but certainly not least, I would like to express my gratitude to my wife Diane for her hard work, support and patience.

Needless to say, I am solely responsible for any errors of fact and logic.

Mehran Tamadonfar

Introduction

In recent decades, the Islamic revivalist movement has played a pivotal role in the socio-economic and political developments of the Muslim Middle East. This role in disestablishing monarchism in Iran and substituting it with an Islamic regime, intensifying conflicts and wars and augmenting violent and non-violent challenges to the established regimes and their leaders, has finally drawn global attention to the Islamic belief system and its impact upon the future developments of the Islamic world.

In the West, the past neglect of Islam was partly due to the lack of understanding of this belief system and its role and partly to Westerners' preoccupation with developmentalist frameworks that generally dismissed the vital function religion serves in the development of underdeveloped societies. Today, in the interest of formulating an effective response to the Islamic challenge, the non-Islamic world is, more than ever, interested in Islam and acknowledges its global significance. Thanks to this growing interest, currently the Western reader has an unprecedented access to a wealth of literature on various aspects of Islam. Although recently published materials have been informative and conducive to a much better understanding of the Islamic belief system, they unfortunately contain conceptual, methodological and theoretical shortcomings which inadequately describe the complex issues in Islam. There have yet to be developed frameworks that can comprehensively examine the complex and highly-integrated Islamic belief system. It is my contention that the conceptual, methodological and theoretical frameworks of Western social science—in their original forms—are simply inadequate tools for the study of the issues of the developing world. Nevertheless, a total abandonment of these frameworks seems premature. Until we develop a genuine Third World approach, it is imperative to be open to modified versions of those Western frameworks that can be conducive to a better, though not totally comprehensive, understanding of Third World issues. In this book, such frameworks are employed for the study of the Islamic polity and political leadership.

This book is essentially about leadership in Islam. My interest in leadership studies grew out of the realization that studies of developing systems lack adequate consideration of the leadership phenomenon. At least for methodological, theoretical and ideological reasons, students of developed systems have chosen not to attach much significance to leadership. The preoccupation with behavioralism and pluralism in American political science has focused attention on structural issues and has generally downgraded the role of leadership in the development of Western societies. In view of the fact that leaders have always played a major role in both developed and developing societies, it is imperative to reevaluate our tools and examine the ever-significant leadership factor.

In the first chapter, the reader is introduced to the major conceptual, methodological and theoretical problems and explanations in the study of leadership. It is presumed here that any leadership analysis methodologically requires a synthesis of both organismic and mechanistic models. In this method, leaders are not studied in isolation. They are treated as an integral component of the polity involved in a symbiotic influence relationship with their environment. Thus, the study of leadership entails the study of leaders' qualities, their environments and leader-environment interactions.

Two Western theoretical frameworks seem appropriate for the study of Islamic political leadership—namely, elite theories and theories of charismatic authority. As in elite theories, Islam accepts the unavoidability of social stratification and accounts for leadership as an integral component of the polity. Theories of charismatic authority are applicable to the Islamic polity since they attach a unique significance to the individual attributes of the leaders. In Islam, the primary source of leaders' legitimacy is their charismatic qualities that enable them to come to power and lead the community in the divinely-inspired direction. In the first chapter, these theories are examined in some detail.

The second chapter is allocated to the study of the Islamic polity which is the context or environment of leadership in Islam. Here, the Islamic political, economic and social systems as well as policies are studied. In spite of the juridical and sectarian schisms over certain political and theological issues, there is apparently a basic consensus among Muslims about the essential features of the Islamic polity. Classic and modern Muslim thinkers have insisted that a polity is Islamic only if it is founded upon and committed to the implementation of Islamic principles. This proposition raises two fundamental questions: one, has there ever been a complete and genuine Islamic polity in the post-Muhammad era; and two, is such a polity an Islamic utopia that is unattainable? Answers to these questions are neither easy nor are they satisfactory. Historically speaking, many regimes—monarchic and republican—have claimed to be Islamic and to one degree or another have committed themselves to the implementation of certain Islamic principles. Their opponents have questioned the Islamic nature and thus the legitimacy of these regimes. For instance, many have criticized existing regimes governing Muslim societies, including the Iranian and Pakistani regimes that are officially considered Islamic, for being established on non-Islamic principles and for their insensitivity to the basic premises of Islam. It is evident that despite specific Islamic rulings regarding the polity, in practice the parameters of the Islamic polity is currently defined by power holders, a majority of whom are either not committed to the establishment of an Islamic system or maintain a limited view of what constitutes an Islamic polity.

With the growing influence of Islamic forces in Muslim societies, there is a renewed popular commitment to the establishment of a genuine Islamic system. This has encouraged a continuing debate about the structural and functional features of this system and the types of policies that it will pursue. In this book, not every system that governs Muslims is presumed to be Islamic. Rather, as generally understood by Muslims, it is suggested here that an Islamic system is one that is founded upon and committed to the implementation of Islamic principles. Without suggesting whether such a system is viable or not, and by relying upon a number of classical and modern thinkers, this book examines the basic features of the Islamic polity. For example, it suggests that the Islamic political system is monolithic rather than pluralistic and prefers fusion or limited separation of powers over a radical separation of powers. It also asserts that while the Islamic economic and social systems attempt to establish an egalitarian society, they acknowledge some degree of inequality.

Although Islam is theoretically a monolithic ideology intent on establishing an order on the basis of common Islamic values, soon after the prophet Muslims developed divergent views on the issue of authority. This political schism, which began with disputes over the issue of succession to the prophet, gradually entailed differences over more fundamental political and subsequently theological issues leading to disintegrating sectarian tendencies that have continued to date. These tendencies have resulted in the formulation of distinct sectarian doctrines and practices of authority in Islam, making it practically impossible to examine Islamic leadership without consideration for Islamic sectarianism. In the third chapter, the roots, evolution and political implications of Islamic sectarianism is addressed. It is proposed that sectarianism originated from disputes over political questions, developed into profound disagreements over theological and political doctrines and practices, and continues to divide the Islamic community.

Given the impact of sectarianism on the theory and practice of authority, the fourth chapter comparatively analyzes the Sunni and Shi'i theories and practice of leadership. It is argued here that although the two doctrines of *khalifah* and *imamah* were distinct, the Sunni practice of leadership resembled some of the Shi'i doctrinal positions and leadership as practiced in most traditional—patriarchal and patrimonial—polities. The Sunni doctrine of *khalifah* that originally bestowed broad-ranging political and spiritual responsibilities on the caliph and accounted for popular input in his choice and the manner by which he governs communal affairs, was gradually modified to reflect the practical necessities of the community. Thus, for instance, later additions to the doctrine of *khalifah* accommodated the notion of separation of temporal authority from the spiritual one and accepted inheritance and force as sources of the caliph's legitimacy. Historically speaking, as the early patriarchal caliphs were succeeded by patrimonial ones, the Sunni caliphs gradually abanoned their spiritual role and solely functioned as the temporal authority in the Islamic community. Furthermore, in managing communal affairs they essentially relied on a selected few rather than the community at large, making it simply impossible for the community to have an effective input in the decision-making process.

Underscoring the legitimist argument which stresses the right of the prophet's family to the leadership of the community, Shi'is developed doctrines of *imamah* that have essentially remained unchanged. Despite practical necessities to modify some of the fundamental principles of these doctrines, Shi'is have generally maintained the basic premises of the *imamah* doctrines and have insisted on an appointive process for leadership succession. While only Ali actually ruled the community, Shi'ism that occasionally pursued either a quietist or an activist approach to authority never abandoned its legitimist stand. Shi'i leaders continued to claim political and spiritual authority, and even those who favored quietism did so for self-preservation and/or the protection of Shi'ism rather than an actual rejection of the imams' right to authority. Shi'i factions have, however, failed to develop a general theory of leadership for their post-*imamah* era. Whereas some fundamentalist Twelvers openly reject any authority but that of the Hidden Imam—Mahdi—others insist that in the absence of this imam there is a need for some form of authority. However, they sharply differ over the nature of leadership during this stage. Some advocate a democratic system involving popular participation, others favor an elitist system that entitles a few learned individuals to rule. In this final chapter, the roots, developments and theoretical and practical implications of these theories are examined in detail.

1

A Framework for Analysis

THE STUDY OF LEADERSHIP: SIGNIFICANCE AND STATUS

The vital role of political leaders in predominantly patrimonial developing systems and the current rise in the power of political executives in many developed systems warrant a systematic study of political leadership in contemporary political science. Leadership studies gain more significance as political scientists gradually recognize that the study of ". . . 'Third World' politics cannot be limited to structural analyses but must give due consideration to the impact of leadership variable."[1] The study of developed systems requires a similar approach due to the rapid rise in the power of their political leaders in the twentieth century and the contributions of these leaders to the establishment and maintenance of democratic societies.

Despite this recognition, no systematic approach to the study of leadership has been developed. Currently, attempts at developing such a method present a challenge to the entire discipline of political science. According to Glenn Paige,

> The challenge is to recognize the importance of political leadership, to focus scientific attention upon it, and to begin the cumulative process of conceptualization, theory building, empirical research, education, application, and institutionalization that eventually will lead to the creation of a sub-disciplinary and potentially transdisciplinary scientific field of global significance.[2]

This challenge has not been met effectively. The status of leadership studies may accurately be summed up as "past neglect, present emergence, and future potential."[3] The present uneasiness with, or even neglect of, leadership phenomenon in American political science may be explained by the general intellectual and political climate in the profession, which attributes political development to the influence of socio-economic forces rather than individual leaders; and its preoccupation with behavioralism and group approach, which might be methodologically and even theoretically irreconcilable with leadership studies. As Lewis Edinger points out, behavioralism's concern with the scientific study of politics requires strict adherence to empirical methods of conceptualization, observation and testing. The effective application of these methods to leadership analysis requires further development in these areas as well as a broad range of other tasks that are currently impeding a scientific study of political leadership.[4]

The current debate over the methodological orientations of the discipline has drawn attention to the issue of substance versus method. Specifically, are we prepared to ignore the significance of such societal phenomena as leadership in response to conceptual, methodological and theoretical shortcomings of behavioralism? Is it possible to devise methods that allow for the systematic investigation of these phenomena without abandoning the basic principles and premises of behavioralism?

Currently a rigorous application of behavioralism to the study of leadership is exceedingly difficult. However, as Edinger astutely observes, behavioralism is not totally irreconcilable with leadership studies if we bring to bear upon these studies ". . . some of the findings and methods of the behavioral approach in a less restrictive manner than is now practiced in a conscious attempt to be 'scientific.'" Methodologically speaking, leadership can be studied by frameworks which incorporate empirical methods and "the disciplined application of imaginative thinking."[5]

This approach should by no means be limited to leadership studies. Actually, the study of any socio-political phenomenon requires such a flexibility in search of more applicable frameworks.

TOWARD A CONCEPTUAL, METHODOLOGICAL AND THEORETICAL FRAMEWORK

Conceptualization

Most social science concepts suffer from some degree of ambiguity that can be attributed to their lack of clear and commonly accepted definitions. This so-called conceptual confusion has been an impediment to the progress of the social sciences. A major difficulty in advancing the discipline of political science, according to Giovanni Sartori, has been its conduciveness ". . . to indefiniteness, to undelimited and largely undefined conceptualizations."[6] The continuing introduction of competing conceptualizations compounds this problem.

As in the natural sciences, the first step in the advance of the social sciences towards paradigmatic achievements seems to be a commitment to conceptual consensus and clarity. The use of common words in technical contexts, as suggested by some, not only does not facilitate clarity of concepts, it actually adds to the delusion of sufficiency and confusion by similarity. These compounding problems present serious obstacles to the systematic study of social phenomena, a study which requires both clear and operational concepts. Recent attempts at conceptual clarification have lagged ". . . behind the development and application of methodological techniques used in operationalizing concepts."[7]

No central definition for the concept of leadership has yet been developed. According to James MacGregor Burns, a recent study has turned up one hundred and thirty definitions of this concept.[8] Perhaps, this is attributed partly to the ambiguity of the "intuitive notion of leadership,"[9] and partly to those leadership scholars who ". . . have worked in separate disciplines and subdisciplines in pursuit of different and often unrelated questions and problems."[10] Despite the lack of consensus over a general and explicit definition of this concept, students of leadership basically define leadership in terms of a relationship. The relational nature of leadership is underscored when leadership is essentially defined as a process or a situation. Relation is the core of Burns' definition when he suggests,

> Leadership is the reciprocal process of mobilizing, by persons with certain motives and values, various economic, political, and other resources, in a context of competition and conflict, in order to realize goals independently or mutually held by both leaders and followers.[11]

While the relational aspect of leadership is agreed upon, the types and nature of this relationship are the source of disagreements. Generally speaking, leadership may be defined as a relationship involving power, influence and authority. Lester Seligman's typology of leadership relations[12] and Burns' recognition of the "symbiotic"[13] nature of leadership relationships illustrate the significance of power, influence, authority, command and control in this relationship.[14] Some scholars, like Burns, have excluded coercive forms of power and influence from leadership relationships. Dictatorial rule, from this viewpoint, is not a form of leadership because, as Burns asserts, leaders induce ". . . followers to act for certain goals that represent the values and the motivations—the wants and needs, the aspirations and expectations—of both leaders and followers."[15]

Defining leadership only in the context of the use of legitimate power, when the power holder is perceived to have the right to prescribe behavior for other group members to follow, clearly limits the leadership relationship to non-coercive influence patterns. Exclusion of dictatorial rule from the realm of leadership is undesirable, unreal and misleading since it limits the scope of leadership relationships. Accurately observed by Robert Tucker, "a leadership approach to politics must not rule out by its terms of reference the phenomenon of authoritarian or dictatorial leadership."[16] Edwin Hollander, who believes that a leadership process usually involves a symbiotic influence relationship aimed at attaining mutual goals, also admits that the leadership relationship involves both persuasion and coercion.[17]

The conceptual problem is compounded when one is dealing with a particular type of leadership such as political leadership. Defining the term *politics* is probably as difficult as defining *leadership*, if not more so. If politics is defined in terms of power, as power theoreticians do, political leadership—as any other type of leadership—may be defined as a type of relationship involving power. However, this perspective is accurately criticized for its conceptual ambiguity, methodological inadequacies and theoretical implications. As understood by Tucker, Plato equated politics with leadership itself. From this viewpoint, which is a contrast to the power school argument, politics in essence is leadership, or attempted leadership, of whatever is the prevailing form of political community.[18]

Methodology

As suggested earlier, our limited ability to study leadership systematically impedes the recognition and development of leadership studies. In order to overcome some of these limitations, students of leadership should be able to find some answers to the following methodological questions:

1. What is leadership?
2. Who are the leaders?
3. How should leadership be studied?

The difficulty with the concepts is both definitional and operational. Students of leadership have not agreed upon definitions and, subsequently, have not been successful in operationalizing concepts. Even if clear definitions are adopted, there is no guarantee that concepts can be easily operationalized in a research strategy. The result, as Kenneth Janda suggests, is that "little comparability exists among leadership studies in the aggregate, for these studies, being guided by widely differing notions of the phenomenon called leadership, have not concerned themselves with common phenomena."[19]

Edinger has proposed three methods to operationalize the concept of leadership. They are the positional-ascriptive method, which is a traditional method that attempts to identify leaders on the basis of the official position of the individuals; the behavioral-descriptive method, which focuses on the individual's performance rather than position; and the cognitive-attitudinal method, which identifies individual leaders based on subjective perception of their role rather than their actual behavior.[20]

Although a combination of these methods can effectively assist us in identifying political leaders, they still leave major methodological difficulties unresolved. Certainly, the scope of leadership studies should be much broader than the study of individual leaders' backgrounds, personalities and policy preferences. Since leadership is defined in terms of relationships, the study of leadership should involve not only the leaders but also the network of their interactions with each other and their followers. Hollander's Transactional and Paige's Multivariate, Multidimensional Linkage approaches account for the study of these multiple relationships.

Hollander's Transactional approach attempts to study leadership by examining,

> ... the relationship of three elements, each complex within itself. These are the "leader" with his or her personality, perceptions, and resources relevant to goal attainment; the "followers" with their personalities, perceptions, and relevant resources; and the situation within which all these persons function.[21]

In this model, the "locus of leadership" is where the leader and followers are bound together in a relationship within a situation. Similar importance is attached to "situations" in other approaches that can be characterized as contextual. According to Seligman, a useful approach ". . . is the one that centers always on the power and policy context of leadership behavior."[22] Also, as Dankwart Rustow states,

> the study of leadership, moreover, can readily be supplemented with an examination of the social and political organization that he founds and transforms, with an analysis of the psychological appeals and political sanctions that give leader and organization a hold on their mass following.[23]

These systematic and comprehensive approaches might methodologically reconcile the mechanistic and organismic theoretical models of leadership studies, assist conceptual clarity and operationalization and lead to some consensus over the scope of these studies. However, they are unable to resolve many other major difficulties in research performance. For instance, despite significant progress in survey research techniques and statistical methods for data analysis, problems such as leaders' inaccessibility and subsequent data unreliability or insufficiency always remain major impediments to the scientific study of leadership.

Theoretical Models: A Synthesis

A major theoretical question in leadership studies is whether or not scientific methods are capable of producing systematically related generalizations about leadership that allow for new observations and testing. Burns' answer to this question is positive since he insists that,

> In the billions of acts that comprise the leadership process, or parts of it, a pattern can be discerned that makes possible generalizations about leadership, generalizations that in turn would underlie an effective general theory and serve as a guide to the successful practice of leadership.[24]

These generalizations, in his view, can be made across polities and over time because of the availability of concepts and data.

This view, however, is not shared by many students of leadership. According to Donald Searing, the challenge of leadership theory construction is confounded by two often dogmatic controversies: the great man-social forces dispute in individual leadership studies, and the pluralist-stratification debate in elite research. Drawing upon these controversies, Searing presents two models, one mechanistic and the other organismic, for the study of individual leaders and elites. The primary distinction between these models is their dichotomous approaches to society and the nature of its components. Therefore, the degree to which these two models are applied to leadership across polities and over time depends upon their societal contexts. In the words of Searing, ". . . in some situations great men are likely important, pluralism viable, and mechanistic models most appropriate. In other situations social forces prevail, stratification is more likely the rule, and organismic models are most reliable."[25]

In mechanistic models the society is presumed to consist of a set of constant and discrete sub-systems dominated by the leadership sub-system. A methodological implication of this theoretical assumption is that the study of leadership, the sub-system, gains precedence over the study of its societal context—the whole system. In this approach, ". . . the leader's actions are explained more by the internal psychological sources of his behavior, than by the influence of the systemic leadership context."[26]

Mechanistic models do not, however, totally deny the impact of the societal context on leadership. Leaders' greatness, in William Ogburn's view, must be conceived ". . . in terms of inherited qualities and environmental traits." Thus, their influence ". . . depends not only on their talent but also on the favorableness of the social conditions."[27] Great men, in this perspective, shape and are shaped by their environments. The degree of influence each has—the great man and his environment—in this symbiotic relationship is relative to place and time.

Historicists like Hegel, Spencer and Marx oppose the mechanistic models because they believe that leaders are little more than ciphers in an inevitable historical progression. While these men disagree on the features and meaning of this historical progression, they do agree that leaders are unable to manipulate it. Thus, in this deterministic perspective, the heroic leader cannot be more than a catalyst for events, which would have occurred with or without these personalities.[28]

Unlike mechanistic models, organismic models assume that components of the society are highly interdependent and relate to each other by processes of evolutionary social change. These models are system dominant and aid the study of leadership in its systemic context, a context that ". . . shapes recruitment parameters, and molds the roles the leader can play."[29] Plato, Gaetano Mosca and Vilfredo Pareto treated society as an organismic whole. Plato's Republic exhibited a highly integrated system consisting of units which would perform their natural functions as part of a unified and organic whole. "Since integration facilitates communication and control," Plato concluded, "the Republic's elite-mass relationships could easily be controlled by a cohesive group of philosopher kings."[30] Aristotle criticized the unreality of Plato's organismic model, and presented a mechanistic model with less integration and greater competition among groups.

By stressing interdependence and integration, organismic models advocate evolutionary rather than revolutionary change. Furthermore, methodologically speaking, they facilitate the study of the system as a whole since in their approach ". . . socio-economic factors are often accorded primacy in determining relations among the parts."[31] According to Searing, two sets of relationships can be studied in organismic elite research: the intra-elite relationship, which explains the internal characteristics of governing elites; and the elite-mass relationship, which explains the relations of the rulers and the ruled.

It should be stressed that many leadership models are spread out along the continuum between organismic and mechanistic poles. All of these models combine certain aspects of these poles so that an appropriate mix of individual and societal considerations are included in the study of certain leadership phenomena. Thus, for every single leadership and elite research project, appropriate models should be designed to facilitate the study of leadership in its respective context.

SELECTED WESTERN THEORETICAL FRAMEWORKS FOR THE STUDY OF ISLAMIC POLITICAL LEADERSHIP

Any systematic approach to societal phenomena requires certain theoretical guidelines to promote effective frameworks for research. A systematic analysis of the Islamic political leadership should rely on theories that reflect the premises of a methodology which synthesizes organismic and mechanistic models of leadership studies. Therefore, these theories should not only allow for the study of the leadership context—a highly integrated context involving leadership interactions with other components of the society—but also leaders' individual qualities.

Although one might convincingly argue that Western theories of leadership are inappropriate tools for the study of the Islamic political leadership, it is my contention that the basic premises of elite theories and theories of charismatic authority are not totally alien to Islamic political thought, and thus are at least partly applicable to the Islamic political leadership.

Elite Theories

Historically, elite theories have never gained widespread popularity in the West. In the twentieth century, the effective eclipse of these theories in those countries where they had previously achieved some degree of acceptance mainly originated from the historical experiences of Western societies in the latter part of the nineteenth and the first half of the twentieth centuries. These historical experiences raised fundamental philosophical questions regarding social problems and policy choices in these societies. Welfare-statism of the post WWII era was a policy response to such problems.

This orientation directed scholarly attention to the society at large rather than the elites. Consequently, the remaining interest in elite theories gradually disappeared and "as the post-war period proceeded, fewer and fewer people could be found who were prepared to revert to, or even grudgingly concede the partial validity of, elitist hypothesis."[32] The trend towards welfare-statism and ideologism, and the disregard for elitism, adversely affected the scholarly study of many socio-political phenomena, including social change and transformation. Elite theories

The Elite Concept

Embedded in the concept of elite and elite theories is the idea of social stratification which presumes that all societies consist of a minority of elites who govern and a majority of non-elites who are governed. This concept closely parallels the concept of class and its variations. However, the two concepts that bear certain similarities are not totally identical. George D. H. Cole and Suzanne Keller differentiated the two concepts of ruling class and strategic elites. According to Keller, the strategic elite may be thought of as further differentiation of a ruling class. "In sum, strategic elites differ from a ruling class in their manner of recruitment, internal organization, and degree of specialization."[33]

The etiology of the term "elite" is to be found in the Latin word "eligere" meaning "to choose." Ordinarily, elite refers to choice-makers and to persons occupying high positions. In the social sciences, "the emphasis has shifted from that of choiceness to eminence."[34] Today, trait and functional definitions of the concept can be found in social and political writings. The trait definition emphasizes the qualities of individuals who hold elite status in the society. The functional definition is based on the utility and function of the individual elite in the society.

In trait definitions usually a particular field of eminence is selected as the main criterion for distinguishing elites from non-elites. In this perspective, elites are ". . . in essence constituted on a basis of some sort of personal capacity . . ."[35] Amitai Etzioni and Harold Lasswell emphasize power capacity as the main criterion. According to Etzioni, elites are "groups of actors who have power."[36] In Lasswell's later definition, the political elite consists of the power holders of a body politic.[37]

The trait and functional definitions are not mutually exclusive. Lasswell's emphasis on the functional importance of elite power explicitly makes his definition a functional one as well. Pareto presented both trait and functional definitions. The concept of elite, in his view, ". . . should be treated as a value-free term meaning those who score highest on scales measuring any social value or commodity ("utility"), such as power, riches, knowledge."[38] His definition is functional when he relies on the criterion of position for defining the concept of governing elite. Carl Friedrich also defines elites both in terms of their traits (power) and functions (ability to monopolize rule in a community).[39] Saint-Simon relied solely on a functional definition of elite. According to him, elites are those who perform ". . . the tasks which are indispensable to economic prosperity and scientific progress . . ."[40]

The idea of elite plurality is embedded in most functional definitions. Among others, Saint-Simon, Lasswell, Pareto and P. de Rousiers accepted the plurality of elites. For example, Saint-Simon discussed scientific elites, economic organizers and cultural-religious elites; Lasswell distinguished between political and non-political elites; Pareto talked about governing and non-governing elites; and de Rousiers identified three main elite functions and their corresponding elites: economic, intellectual-cultural, and political.[41]

Theoretical Models

Elite theories are not new. A host of philosophers, from Aristotle and Plato to Karl Mannheim and Lasswell, have developed explanations for elite emergence and proliferation, cohesion and polarization, functions, recruitment, relationships and circulation. Although their theories may be categorized as either functional or trait-motivational perspectives, most involve some aspects of each.

The functionalist perspective advocated by Plato and Aristotle was based on the assumption that the state's functions are to fulfill collective ends and to serve communal needs. To perform these functions, Aristotle argued that the state needs men of virtue and excellence who value justice and the common interest above private gain. In this perspective, the emergence of elites is due to their functional contributions to the society irrespective of the form of government. Saint-Simon understood this interconnection between elites and social functions more clearly than Aristotle.

A combination of trait-motivational and functional perspectives appear in works by Mosca and Pareto. In their works, as in Saint-Simon's, social stratification and elite emergence is attributed to human nature and the functional necessities of the society. Both Mosca and Pareto viewed the elites as the ". . . 'best' people—best, that is, in terms of the values of the society at a given time."[42] As clearly expressed by Mosca and Pareto, elite leadership is inevitable due to elite attributes and functions and the inherent nature of society. According to Mosca,

> Among the constant facts and tendencies that are to be found in all political organisms, one is so obvious that it is apparent to the most casual eye. In all societies—from societies that are very meagerly developed and have barely attained the dawnings of civilization, down to the most advanced and powerful societies—two classes of people appear—a class that rules and a class that is ruled. The first class, always the less numerous, performs all political functions, monopolizes power and enjoys the advantages that power brings, whereas the second, the more numerous class, is directed

and controlled by the first, in a manner that is now more or less legal, now more or less arbitrary and violent . . .⁴³

Unlike Aristotle who foresaw government by one, by the few or by the many, Mosca was of the opinion that government is always the product of an organized minority which imposes itself by ethical force on an unorganized majority. The organized nature of the minority may be attributed to its size and the superior qualities of its members who ". . . have some attribute, real or apparent, which is highly esteemed and very influential in the society in which they live."⁴⁴ In his later works, Mosca downgraded the roles of force and fraud in facilitating minority control and emphasized their "representativeness." According to him, in modern times, this minority is intimately connected with the society through a sub-elite of civil servants, managers and other white collar workers, scientists, scholars and intellectuals, and in some sense represents the interests and purposes of important and influential groups in the society. The qualities and roles of this sub-elite is of vital importance for the preservation of the systemic stability.

Mosca was clearly the first to make a systematic distinction between these two strata in the society without referring to them as elites and non-elites. Pareto, however, first referred to this minority as the elites, and identified three groups in the society: the governing elite or class, the non-governing elite, and the non-elite class or masses. Regardless of the constitutional forms, he asserted, any system consists of a minority who rules and a majority who is ruled.

Despite Mosca's and Pareto's common views on the origins of elites, which led Renzo Sereno to conclude that "Mosca was the founder of the 'political class' theory, and the theory of elite by Pareto is nothing more than Mosca's theory with some of its elements emphasized, some of its points amplified, and its fundamental name changed,"⁴⁵ the two differed fundamentally over the elite-follower relationship. Mosca's later writings discussed the notions of "sub-elites" and "representation" and consequently distinguished between modern political democracy and previous modes of rule. Paretoan theory, however, never made such a distinction and ". . . dismissed every form of 'government of the people' as a mere sham."⁴⁶

Elite Emergence and Proliferation. Robert Michels and C. Wright Mills viewed functional specialization in the society as the primary source of elite emergence. Unlike Pareto, Michels and Mills did not explain elite emergence and domination as a consequence of human nature. According to Michels' "iron-law of oligarchy," the emergence of an oligarchy and the oligarchy's conflicts with its followers is due to the inevitability of stratification within any organization. As he observed, "who says organization, says oligarchy."[47] Michels argued that it is not the organization itself, but the organization's need for leadership that is conducive to oligarchy.[48] In his view, stratification and functional specialization are inevitable in democracies, since they involve large numbers which require organization and specialization in order to synchronize activities.

Mannheim, whose functionalist perspective of elitism helped him to view elites as an integral part of a system of collective relationships and needs, emphasized elite proliferation rather than elite decline in advanced industrial societies. Elite proliferation, in his view, is due to elite functions. The nature of these functions rather than the motives of power-hungry individuals determine the constitution of elites. Although elite leadership is inevitable and necessary, it is increasingly exercised within the context of specific institutions and consequently more limited and, hence, more legitimate.[49]

Historically, elites appeared in those societies where some degree of division of labor and, consequently, a system of class stratification was accepted. In ancient societies, where division of labor led to class stratification, higher classes were exempt from agricultural work and became both superior to, and completely dependent upon, the lower classes who performed such work. Elites grew out of the further division of the stratified society ". . . and the dichotomy between its management and the total membership."[50] The affinity between the elites and the upper class, as two components of an interdependent network, grew stronger as a result of their mutual interests.

Elites emerge and proliferate in the society irrespective of the society's constitutional framework and the level of development. They are found within totalitarian and democratic political frameworks as well as traditional and modern societies. Generally speaking, four main social processes, according to Keller, are conducive to elite emergence and proliferation: the growth of population; the growth of occupational specialization; the growth of formal organization, or bureaucracy; and the growth of moral diversity among the populace, which is partly due to the growing gap between the core values of the society and the personal values of its individual members. In her view, modern industrial societies manifest elite emergence and proliferation due to their antecedent historical conditions, currently operative social forces and the functional requirements of large scale social systems.[51]

Elite Cohesion and Polarity. A number of elite theories, especially the ones by Pareto, Mosca and Mills, have been criticized for assuming elite homogeneity and cohesion. According to Friedrich, in democracies elites do not constitute a cohesive group due to their changing composition.[52] Mills' elites constitute a cohesive group, but most theorists have accepted the notion of elite polarity. Pareto himself contended that "there is never, to be exact, one elite stratum, there are only various strata which together constitute the elites."[53]

The degree of elite cohesion and polarity depends upon the nature of the elite groups and their context. Intellectual, bureaucratic and managerial elites, for example, are generally considered polarized; while military, political, scientific and business elites have basically revealed a great degree of uniformity and cohesion. The levels of socio-economic, political and scientific development only partly determine the degree of elite cohesion and polarity. G. Lowell Field and John Higley's historical-developmental approach has concluded that the kind of elite is partly determined by the society's development level and mainly by the occurrence or non-occurrence of particular types of rather rare historical events.[54]

The nature of a political system and its stability in part depend upon the degree of cohesion among its elites and the essence of their relationship with their followers. According to Field and Higley, even an imperfect consensual unity among elites is preferable to ideological unity in pursuit of systemic stability, because consensual unity, unlike ideological unity, tends to moderate intra-elite and elite-follower conflicts. In the long run, however, an ideologically unified elite can deliberately move toward a consensual unity and enhance systemic stability.[55] Elite polarity facilitates non-elites' control over the elites and consequently enhances democracy. As Keller points out, "the heterogeneity of elites has also contributed to the decline of direct coercion and the rise of persuasion, a striking characteristic of industrial societies."[56]

The Elite-Follower Relationship. Major classic writers advocated the idea of elite determinacy and the lack of checks and controls over their actions. Mosca, Michels, Alexis de Tocqueville and George Simmel, among others, however, believed that elites should be both responsible and responsive to their followers. The consequent reciprocal relationship, which does not necessarily imply an identity of aims and actions between elites and followers, is conducive to democracy. The absence of this reciprocity accounts for the oppressive tyranny that might be exercised by the elites over their followers.

Higley and Field's study, which concludes that the elite-follower relationship varies at different levels of development, presents strong proof for reciprocity by arguing that elites are always in need of followers' support and consequently bound by followers' wishes which are expressed in general terms. Due to the generality of followers' views, the elite is left with making choices that have to reflect the followers' wishes in order to guarantee the continuity of the elite's power and tenure.[57] The same study concludes that the level of socio-economic development not only affects the intra-elite relationship, but also greatly influences the elite-follower relationship. Developed societies tend to have differentiated and specialized elites whose interests and aims are not fully identical with their followers. This lack of identity of interests and aims might very well lead to conflict in the elite-follower relationship.[58] The elites' effective persuasive capabilities combined with the followers' limited knowledge of and information about politics could lead to despotism and uncontrollable elites. Thus, despotism can be partly attributed to followers. Undoubtedly, "indifference and apathy, the incapacity to criticize, and a tendency to turn leaders into idols may make the masses as 'responsible' for a despotic leader as the propensities of the leaders themselves." Superior knowledge and the cult of gratitude increases the leaders' conviction of infallibility and contempt for followers to the extent that leaders "proclaim both the sovereignty of the masses and the incompetence of the people."[59] Despotism might also stem from the counsel of leaders' advisors.

In today's Western democracies, however, despotism faces a number of limitations such as increased public control over the elites through non-elite participation; specialization of authority, which constricts the range of power; and the narrowing gap between leaders and their followers with respect to education, standard of living, and general well-being.[60]

Elite Functions. Reciprocity in the elite-follower relationship contributes to the efficiency of the elite function which, in general terms, involves directing the followers at times of choice and change. A leader, according to Plato, ". . . is one who gives direction to a collective's activities."[61] Elites' directive functions consist of three interrelated functions: a diagnostic function, whereby elites define the situation authoritatively for their followers; a prescriptive/policy-formulating function, which is prescribing a course of action that will meet the situation as defined; and a mobilizing/policy-implementing function, which is gaining the followers' support for the definition of the situation, the decisions to act and the implementation of actions.[62]

The policy implication of reciprocity in the elite-follower relationship is the achievement of some type of balance between elite preferences and policies and the desires of the masses. Reciprocity also affects the manner by which leaders define and pursue societal goals. Although the revolutionary and reformist leaders' goal is to bring about change, the reformer ". . . characteristically seeks change by gradual and peaceful tactics that emphasize persuasion, whereas the revolutionary seeks change by extremist tactics that include violence."[63] Of course, the revolutionary leader might adopt reformist strategies and the reformist might pursue revolutionary tactics. Moreover, the reform leader strives to preserve the society's myths and ideal cultural patterns, while the revolutionary leader calls for a fundamental reconstruction of the society.

Elite Recruitment. The socio-economic and political characteristics of the society and the essence of the leader-follower relationship also determine the patterns of elite recruitment. Historically speaking, elite recruitment has been based on two contending principles: ascriptiveness, which presumes superiority of biological and social inheritance; and meritocracy, which stresses the achieved attributes and demonstrated merits of elite contenders. Although contending, ascriptiveness and meritocracy have found an easy truce and have become ". . . integrated, in varying ways, into the basic value systems of societies . . ."[64] While the numerical growth of elites and their increased specialization have been instrumental in the spread of meritocracy, ascriptiveness is still an elite recruitment pattern in modern societies.

Having these two patterns in mind, Keller presents at least seven different mechanisms for elite recruitment:

1. Biological reproduction, most common in hereditary monarchic systems;
2. Co-optation to elite ranks, the choice of successor by ruling elites;
3. Election;
4. Election by rote, the choice of elites by a fixed numerical principle;
5. Purchase of elite positions;
6. Forcible appropriation; and
7. Training and formal preparation for elite positions.

These mechanisms can be grouped into three general procedures: hereditary succession; appointment from the top; and election from below. None of these procedures is intrinsically superior or inferior to others, since their legitimacy in a particular system depends upon their functional consistency with the socio-cultural and political aspects of that society. For instance, hereditary succession provides for elite cohesion, continuity and commitment to traditional norms. Therefore, hereditary succession normally enjoys greater legitimacy and is appropriate for traditional monarchic systems. Meritocracy, whether through appointment or election, facilitates upward mobility, broadens and diversifies the elite group and, thus, has greater acceptability in modern societies. Whereas hereditary procedure offers continuity and stability in traditional societies, meritocracy promotes responsiveness to challenge and change in modern societies. Meritocracy, however, might result in elite individualism and competitiveness and lead to incoherence in elites' programs and perspectives which could be socially destructive.[65]

Elite Circulation. Systemic stability and change not only depend upon the patterns of the elite-follower relationship, elite functions and elite recruitment, but also the patterns of change in the composition of elite groups. Pareto's famous remark that "history is a graveyard of aristocracies" clearly testifies to the inevitability of the rise and fall of the elites. Elite theorists, however, do not all agree on the reasons for elite circulation and the manners by which this occurs. Elite circulation has been attributed to sociological, psychological and biological factors. Influenced by the Marxist idea of social change, Mosca attributed elite circulation partly to the emergence of social forces which represent new interests in the society. Elite circulation occurs, Mosca asserted, because "with every new need, new social forces rise to meet the challenge and to ask [for] their share of power of the old established interests."[66] Unlike Pareto, he referred to psychological explanations for elite circulation, but did not attach supreme importance to it. These psychological factors, in his view, are produced by both social circumstances as well as new ideals, interests and problems in the society. Although Mosca attributed changes in the elites primarily to social circumstantial changes,[67] he attempted to disassociate his theory from the Marxist theory of social change by downgrading the impacts of economic factors and by emphasizing the influence of moral and religious ideals in social change. This, of course, brings Mosca very close to Weber.

Joseph A. Schumpeter also deals with sociological and psychological explanations for social change.[68] However, Mosca's and Schumpeter's conceptions of social change differ from Pareto's. In Paretoan theory, elite circulation, which is only a movement within the elite stratum, does not lead to a genuine social transformation. "Through all these movements the form of society remains unchanged, since it is defined abstractly as the rule of an elite over the majority of the population," Pareto contended.[69] Conversely, influenced by Marx, Mosca and Schumpeter concluded that elite circulation leads to a real transformation in the society.

Elite circulation, as perceived by Pareto, is both unavoidable and necessary. "The history of man," according to him, "is the history of the continuous replacement of elites: as one ascends, another declines."[70] This replacement, which is the result of changes in the elites' dominant features, involves a struggle between the elites and those who seek to either supersede them or share in their power or honors. Therefore, elites are overthrown only from within and only due to their psychological changes. Once the victory is won, the ascending elite gradually loses its openness and flexibility to rigidity and corruption. Rigidity and corruption foster elite polarization and the elite's subsequent decline.

The descending elite suffers from decay in the quality of their features, while the ascending elite gains in the elements of superior quality.[71]

The process of elite circulation might be a violent one due to the descending elites' confrontational response to the ascending elites despite the descending elites' growing weakness. The first stage in the process of elite circulation involves the decline of the old elites as manifested in their tendency to become soft, mild, and more human—making them less apt to defending their own power—and, at the same time, their unwillingness to lose their rapacity and greed for the good of others.[72] The second stage signifies the rise of new elites due to their superior qualities.

Elite circulation is necessary for systemic equilibrium and stability. According to Pareto, the failure of circulation may lead to the instability of social equilibrium and ultimately to conquest and revolution. Conquest and revolution bring a new elite to power and establish a new equilibrium.[73]

Like Pareto, Michels explained elite circulation by psychological considerations since he contended that "we may regard it as an established historical law that races, legal systems, institutions, and social classes are inevitably doomed to destruction from the moment they or those who represent them have lost their faith in their own future."[74]

Although many have attempted to adduce biological reasons for the decline of elites, none have done so convincingly. The historical decline of elites has been attributed to elite celibacy and sterility, to their gradual enfeeblement, to their nervous and mental exhaustion and to their sexual intermingling with the lower stratum. Pareto, himself, speculated that the decline of hereditary elites originates in the elites' ability to save all their children, including the feeble, whereas the non-elites could save only the strong. This explanation like others, however, does not clarify the reasons for the decline of non-hereditary elites. Even Francis Bacon could not find distinct biological patterns between elites and non-elites.[75] Clearly, the rise and demise of elites cannot be attributed to a single set of factors, but should be explained by a combination of psychological, sociological and political considerations.

Elitism and Marxism

Since elite theories, particularly those of Mosca and Pareto, rose from the Marxist teachings on class and developed as a conscious and explicit critique of Marxism, a brief comparison between Elitism and Marxism seems useful here. Despite profound differences, and the elitists' strong criticisms of determinism in Marxism, both theories are founded on a deterministic view of society. Elitists' social determinism, which is influenced by but different from the Marxist economic determinism, advocates the unavoidability of social stratification. However, unlike Marxists who believe in the unavoidability of social stratification yet reject its necessity, elitists believe social stratification is necessary. This fundamental difference has allowed the two theories to build significantly different models of social change.

These models are also built upon the two unquestionably different concepts of elite and ruling class. While elitists basically define the elite as possessing superior qualities, Marxists primarily define ruling class in economic terms. However, both theories and their respective concepts retain the idea of a powerful minority seeking to dominate a powerless majority. According to Marxists, this struggle continues between the two strata as long as classes exist. But, according to Pareto, this struggle is not between the powerful and the powerless. Instead, it is a continuous struggle between the powerful and their rivals. ". . . as long as there were minorities who rule there would be minorities who seek to rule."[76] Mosca's introduction of the idea of social forces (i.e. important interests in the society) into the discussion of elite circulation brings him uncomfortably close to Marx, although he avoids association with Marxism by de-emphasizing economic factors.

Marxists espouse that a classless society is both possible and desirable. Due to their belief in the unavoidability and necessity of social stratification, elitists reject the feasibility and the desirability of a classless society. Economic interpretation of history, according to elitists, cannot adequately explain the complexity of historical change as Marxists attempt to do.

Elitism and Democratic Thought

Early elite theories were also critical of democratic thought. Specifically, nineteenth century elitism was mostly developed in feudal societies and was intended to "revive ancient ideas of social hierarchy and to erect obstacles to the spread of democratic notions."[77] However, similarities exist between recent elite and democratic thought.

At the theoretical level, elitism and democratic thought are irreconcilable due to elitism's emphasis on social stratification and democracy's preoccupation with equality. Moreover, the elitist principle of minority (elite) rule contradicts the ever-significant democratic principle of majority rule. These differences are not, however, as sharp in practice as they are in theory. Formalistic redefinitions of democracy and the emphasis on elite plurality, competition and accountability reconcile these contradictions even at the theoretical level.[78] According to Schumpeter's democratic elitism, "Democracy means only that the people have the opportunity of accepting or refusing the men who are to rule them."[79] Mannheim, who originally identified elitism with fascism and distinguished it from democratic thought, argued in his later writings that democracy and elitism are compatible because of elite accountability to the masses in democratic societies.[80]

Elite plurality encourages elite accountability and even some degree of equality. Raymond Aron distinguished between democratic and nondemocratic systems by recognizing elite plurality, competition and accountability in democracies when he stated that "the fundamental difference between a society of the Soviet type and one of the Western type is that the former has a unified elite and the latter a divided elite."[81] This elitist view of democracy is criticized by the proponents of the theory of democratic mass participation. In conclusion to his critical examination of issues such as elite competition, openness of elite ranks and elite accountability to the masses, Peter Bachrach finds a substantial number of disagreements between elitism and democratic thought. A major difference between elitists and classical democratic theorists is their divergent approaches to what constitutes and who determines public interest. Contrary to the classical view of democracy which conceives of the public interest in terms of means as well as ends, Bachrach contends, democratic elitist thought unidimensionally defines public interest in terms of the ends. It presumes that ". . . the general interest is realized when governmental policy is in accord with the judgement of the elite."[82] Moreover, elite pluralism does not necessarily produce a competitive situation among elites and consequently does not always ensure democracy, as democratic elitists presume.[83]

Bachrach's self-developmental approach, which presents an explanation of democracy different from democratic elitism and classical democratic theory, also criticizes the assumptions of democratic elitism which state that elite pluralism and consensus are effective safeguards for democracy. Elites, who have substantive conflicting interests, hardly reach a consensus that can effectively safeguard democracy. Even if such a consensus can be reached, according to Bachrach, ". . . it seems doubtful that they could generate sufficient power democratically to restrain the excessive demands and actions of the undemocratic mass and its leaders."[84] Even Schumpeter, who advocates elite plurality and competition as the necessary means for the preservation of democracy, admits that the success of a democratic system depends upon the quality of elites, the scope and nature of political decisions, the skills of the bureaucracy and democratic self control among and by the elites.

T. B. Bottomore criticizes the elite competition perspectives. Democratic elitism, he insists, ignores changes in the structure and composition of elites, their self-conception and their relations with the rest of the population. The development and improvement of democracy, he adds,

> . . . does not depend primarily upon fostering the competition between small elite groups whose activities are carried on in realms far removed from the observation or control of ordinary citizens, but upon creating and establishing the conditions in which a large majority of citizens, if not all citizens, can take part in deciding those social issues which vitally affect their individual lives . . . and in which the distinction between elites and masses are reduced to the smallest possible degree.[85]

An Evaluation

A general evaluation of elite theories illustrates their major conceptual, methodological and theoretical shortcomings. The concept of elite, its equivalents and derivatives are basically ambiguous, inadequate and bear an ideological overtone. Methodologically speaking, the largely spurious use of historical materials outside their historical contexts in the study of elite circulation is inappropriate and misleading. Moreover, approaches to elite circulation have not made a clear distinction between the movements of individuals in the hierarchy and the process of an overall change in the elite system. Conceptual problems and the inability to test empirical observations are fundamental barriers for theory building in elite studies. Even the theoretical value of elite theories is questionable because, as Robert Dahl suggests, ". . . a theory that cannot even in principle be controverted by empirical evidence is not a scientific theory."[86] Elite theories, if theories and not merely a set of hypotheses, are at least incomprehensive and unidimensional in their discussions of the formation, rise and fall of elites.

Theories of Charismatic Authority

The Concept of Charisma

The concept of charisma has undoubtedly been instrumental in the study of leadership in both developed and underdeveloped systems. However, the interdisciplinary use of this concept and its numerous and often contradictory definitions have resulted in conceptual ambiguity and difficulties with concept operationalization and application.

The term "charisma" is of Greek origin and means "gift."[87] In its religious connotation, charisma refers to the ". . . endowment of divine grace."[88] Max Weber's definition refers to the two elements of personal qualities of leaders and their followers' recognition of these qualities and responsiveness to leaders. According to him, charisma is ". . . a certain quality of an individual personality by virtue of which he is set apart from ordinary men and treated as endowed with supernatural, superhuman, or at least specifically exceptional powers or qualities." The followers' acceptance of and responsiveness to a charismatic leader is due to their ". . . complete personal devotion to the possessor of the [charismatic] quality, arising out of enthusiasm, or of despair and hope."[89]

Although the ambiguity in Weber's conception has raised criticisms, particularly in regard to the importance of the followers' recognition and response, charismatic leadership basically involves a relationship between a leader endowed with certain qualities and followers who admire these qualities and respond to his leadership.[90] Some have minimized, if not disregarded, the importance of leaders' personal attributes by arguing that a leadership is charismatic as long as there are those who follow the leader as a charismatic one.[91] The emergence and success of charismatic leaders, from this point of view, are attributed to such variables as time, place and propaganda more so than their personal qualities. Of course, leadership qualities such as the ability to manage and manipulate followers are critical in attaining the necessary responses by the followers.[92]

The main criticisms of the concept of charisma center around the origin of the concept and its limited applicability. Friedrich and Karl Loewenstein, who believe that this concept originated from a religious realm, favor its restrictive interpretation and application. Despite Weber's improper undertaking to transfer this notion to the realm of politics, Loewenstein concludes, the religious realm still remains the fundamental locus of this concept. Thus, this concept has no relevance to the technological mass democracy, and should only be applied to the pre-Cartesian West and to contemporary societies that have not yet broken away from the "magico-religious ambiance."[93] Friedrich is of the opinion that the secular and non-transcendent types of callings, inspirational leadership of the demagogic type, and the like, should not be included in the category of charismatic leadership because, for instance, ". . . Hitlers represent a very different kind of leadership than the founders or even the inspired supporters of a religion." Even psychologically speaking, they fall in different categories, since "totalitarian leaders are typically preoccupied with power, especially organizational power, while the founders of religions are not."[94]

In Rudolph Sohm's *Kirchenrecht* (1892), from which Weber derived the concept of charisma and the theory of charismatic leadership, charismatic leadership was understood to derive from ". . . a transcendent call by a divine being in which both the person called and his followers believe . . ."[95] Weber admitted to the divine origin of charisma by acknowledging that the charismatic bond between the leader and his followers endures only as long as he is the ruler "by the grace of God."[96] He also alluded to such divinity by saying that whenever charisma appears "it constitutes a 'call' in the most emphatic sense of the word, a 'mission' or a 'spiritual duty.'"[97] Therefore, the legitimacy of charismatic leaders rests upon their personal attributes resulting ". . . from the divine *charis* flowing from God to man . . ."[98]

This religious overtone in the concept of charisma does not necessarily make the concept inapplicable to the political realm, since no clear distinction between the two realms can be easily and effectively made by limiting the religious realm to divinity and the political realm to power. The concept of charisma can be applied to the political realm, as Weber did, because ". . . politics and religion interpenetrate in many ways." Since ". . . founders of religion have not invariably been indifferent to consideration of power" and motivations of political leaders vary, the concept of charisma, despite its mythical components, is relevant to political life even in the age of technological mass democracy.[99]

In addition to the previously described definitional problems, the concepts of charisma and charismatic leadership suffer from methodological shortcomings which include operational difficulties and limited applicability. Charismatic leaders cannot easily be distinguished from non-charismatic ones simply on the basis of the Weberian formulation. This problem is at least partly due to the fact that Weber did not prepare a list of charismatic qualities.

Theoretical Models

Studies of charismatic authority are mostly carried out in the context of the study of change and development. The Weberian theory developed an explanation for the cyclical pattern of change in authority by concluding that societies undergo a sequence of three pure types of charismatic, rational-legal and traditional authorities in their developmental process. In this developmental path, which involves both revolutionary and evolutionary changes of authority, the routinization and bureaucratization of charismatic authority result in the establishment of a rational-legal authority. With the passage of time, rational-legal authority evolves into a traditionalist authority legitimated by usage, precedent and custom. Traditionalism and non-dynamism of this authority in turn facilitate the return of charismatic authority. This pattern of authority change proceeds as societies develop.[100]

Recent functionalist theories of charismatic authority by Edward Shils, David Apter, Dorothy Wilner, Ann Ruth Wilner, George Kahin, Guy Pauker and Lucian Pye also emphasize the pattern of authority change.

In this view, charismatic leadership is a fulcrum of transition from colonial-ruled traditional society to politically independent modern society. Thus, this view historicizes the Weberian sequential pattern ". . . into a sequence that runs from traditional through charismatic to rational-legal forms of authority."[101]

With the gradual withering of people's emotional support for traditional authority, the search for new attachments allows for attitudes conducive to the support of charismatic authority.[102] This explains why charismatic leaders are typically believed to create, or appear in the setting of, dynamic social movements. The leaders' primary functions are the identification of goals, and the mobilization of people's support for these goals and leadership. "To speak of charismatic leaders, then, is to speak of charismatic movements; the two phenomena are inseparable."[103]

Generally speaking, socio-cultural and political settings influence the leader-led relationship. The Weberian argument, however, defines the relationship between leader and follower in the context of traditional religious settings where absolute obedience to authority is the rule; the charismatic leader dominates, thus his followers must obey his orders. The leader's ability to dominate those who follow him originates in his extraordinary qualities, and the followers' obedience arises out of their recognition of the leader as a legitimate enforcer of authority.

Legitimacy of Authority

Leadership legitimacy may be attributed to a multitude of factors. A balanced mix of traditional, Weberian rational-legal and charismatic modes of legitimation is necessary to legitimize authority. Of course this mix of legitimizing sources should coincide with the societal norms. Congruence with societal norms requires dynamism in the legitimacy matrix because legitimizing factors ". . . cannot remain indifferent to changes in the social and economic fabric of society. . . ."[104] The lack of dynamism and adaptability might make a legitimacy crisis unavoidable. As Richard Pfaff has pointed out, "no more revolutionary scenario can be written than that of a regime clinging desperately to a legitimacy matrix in an anachronistic relationship to a changing political culture."[105]

The legitimacy of authority also depends upon the authority's willingness and ability to respond to the societal needs. Followers' needs to overcome their frustrations, to identify with the powerful and to achieve self-esteem; and the charismatic leaders' need for affection, esteem, and self-actualization create a mutual functional dependency in the leader-follower relationship.[106]

Of course, charismatic legitimacy cannot be explained in functional terms alone. It is not only what the leader does or does not do, but also his unique qualities that make a charismatic leader legitimate. Thus far, the study of charismatic qualities has not received systematic attention. Lists of charismatic qualities include a strikingly vivid personality, extreme sensitivity, ability to manipulate the followers, skillful management, extraordinary power of vision, ability to communicate this vision, a sense of mission, self-confidence and faith in success.[107]

An Evaluation

In spite of the disagreements over the scientific worth of the theory of charismatic leadership, there is a growing interest in this subject due to its applicability to certain leadership situations. However, for the theory to develop a broader acceptance it needs to strengthen its conceptual foundation and respond to important methodological questions such as: What are charismatic qualities? How do leaders achieve charismatic qualities? How do followers recognize these qualities? How do these qualities suddenly disappear? Obviously, Weber's contention that charismatic qualities, as non-acquired qualities, are produced in someone through some extraordinary means further confounds these issues. Similarly, at the theoretical level, Weberian analysis of evolutionary change in authority is ambiguous and somewhat inaccurate. Weber would have been more accurate if he had discussed the transformation of charismatic authority into some other form of authority, rather than presuming that through the processes of depersonalization and routinization charisma evolves into either a familial or an institutional charisma. If charisma is a personal attribute, then it cannot be depersonalized, routinized and transferred. In essence, the idea of depersonalization and routinization contradict the basic premise of the theory of charismatic authority.[108]

ELITISM, CHARISMATIC AUTHORITY AND ISLAMIC LEADERSHIP

In the preceding pages, the reader was introduced to the major conceptual, methodological and theoretical issues in the study of elites and individual leaders. The comparative analysis of elitism and democratic and Marxist thoughts was intended to explain the relevance of the elitist framework to the contemporary theories and practices of leadership. Also, it was suggested that the theories of charismatic authority are essentially applicable to leadership in both traditional and modern systems.

To what extent are these frameworks applicable to the study of leadership in Islam? Considering that no social science framework has universal applicability, both elitism and theories of charismatic authority have limited applicability to Islamic political leadership. However, certain premises and principles of both can explain the major theoretical and practical aspects of leadership in Islam.

As in elitism, Islam holds a deterministic view of the society by acknowledging the unavoidability and indispensability of social stratification. Although commitment to equity and justice in Islam necessitates an Islamic community with minimal social distinctions, classic and contemporary Muslim thinkers have generally contended that Islam does indeed believe that social stratification is unavoidable. However, this stratification is not based on economic status or ethno-national features of individuals, rather it is based on their moral attributes and commitments to the Islamic ideology. The Islamic elites—initially, the prophet, the caliphs or imams and their companions; and currently the leader (the imam or *vali-i faqih*) and the clerical establishment—are primarily distinguished from non-elites by their knowledge of Islam, their commitment to the Islamic principles and possession of superior moral values.

Certain components of elite theories, particularly the notion of reciprocity in the elite-follower relationship; the idea of ideological and consensual unity of the elite stratum; and the conceptions of elite circulation and recruitment, especially in their explanations of the modes of succession to power, seem to be helpful in the study of leadership in Islam. In both the Sunni and Shi'i doctrines of leadership, leadership involves a reciprocal relationship between the leader and his followers. This creates a mutual dependency (as also suggested in the theories of charismatic authority) between those who govern and those who are governed. The Islamic doctrine of man's vicegerency to God explicitly refers to this reciprocal relationship.

Ideological harmony and commitment to the implementation of Islamic principles theoretically necessitated a cohesive Islamic elite. However, divergent interpretations of the ideology and a multitude of approaches to political authority polarized the elite stratum in practice. As evident in the sectarian schisms, the two doctrines of *khalifah* and *imamah* and their respective practices culminated in the polarization of the elite stratum and the community as a whole. This fragmentation was intensified with the growing disputes over questions pertaining to the identity of elites, their functions, legitimacy and modes of succession to power. As far as the issue of elite recruitment is concerned, Islam has theoretically emphasized meritocracy. In practice, however, elite recruitment has primarily been based upon ascriptiveness. Perhaps today, more than ever, the Islamic world is troubled with this aspect of leadership, as evident in the Islamic Republic of Iran.

A study of Islamic leadership that synthesizes mechanistic and organismic models of leadership needs to pay utmost attention to leaders' personal attributes (i.e., charisma, etc.) as well as to the environment of Islamic leadership (i.e., the Islamic polity). In view of the fact that the theories of charismatic authority underscore personal attributes of the leader and their contributions to his legitimacy and functional efficacy, these theories provide an exceptionally useful tool for the study of Islamic leadership. In Islam, especially in the Shi'i doctrine of natural right, leadership belongs to those individuals who possess charismatic qualities. Without these qualities, about which Islam is more or less specific, the leader is not considered legitimate and cannot perform his functions effectively. In practice, Islamic leaders have generally been charismatic individuals whose succession to the position of authority and whose ability to maintain their power have mainly depended upon their personal attributes.

In the ensuing chapters, Islamic political leadership is examined by relying on a methodology that synthesizes the organismic and mechanistic models of leadership studies and a theoretical framework that underscores the major elements of elitism and the theories of charismatic authority.

NOTES

1. Paul R. Dettman, "Leaders and Structures in 'Third World' Politics: Contrasting Approaches to Legitimacy," *Comparative Politics* 6 (January 1974): 245.
2. Glenn D. Paige, *The Scientific Study of Political Leadership* (New York: The Free Press, 1977), 1.
3. Ibid., 61.
4. For a detailed discussion of these methodological issues see: Lewis J. Edinger, "Political Science and Political Biography: Reflections on the Study of Leadership (I)," *Journal of Politics* 26 (May 1964): 423-439.
5. Ibid., 436.
6. Giovanni Sartori, "Concept Misformation in Comparative Politics," *American Political Science Review* 64 (December 1970): 1035.
7. Kenneth F. Janda, "Towards the Explication of the Concept of Leadership in Terms of the Concept of Power," *Human Relations* 13 (November 13, 1960): 346.
8. James MacGregor Burns, *Leadership* (New York: Harper and Row, 1978), 2.
9. Kenneth F. Janda, "Towards the Explication of the Concept of Leadership in Terms of the Concept of Power," in *Political Leadership: Readings for an Emerging Field*, ed. Glenn D. Paige (New York: The Free Press, 1972), 55.
10. Burns, *Leadership*, 3.
11. Ibid., 427.
12. Seligman's typology involves four types of relations: "1) the relations of leaders to lead within particular structures, 2) the relationship between leaders of political structures, 3) the relationship between leaders of one structure and

the followers of another, and 4) the relationship between leaders and the 'unorganized' or nonaffiliated." Quoted in Paige, *The Scientific Study of Political Leadership*, 45.

13. Burns, *Leadership*, 452.

14. For a detailed illustration refer to Table 1.1 in Lewis J. Edinger, ed., *Political Leadership in Industrial Societies: Studies in Comparative Analysis* (New York: John Wiley and Sons, 1967), 6-8.

15. Burns, *Leadership*, 19.

16. Robert C. Tucker, *Politics as Leadership* (Columbia: University of Missouri Press, 1981), 12.

17. Edwin P. Hollander, *Leadership Dynamics: A Practical Guide to Effective Relationships* (New York: The Free Press, 1978), 2.

18. Tucker, *Politics as Leadership*, 2-3.

19. Janda, "Towards the Explication of the Concept of Leadership," *Human Relations* 350.

20. Lewis J. Edinger, "Political Science and Political Biography (II): Reflections on the Study of Leadership," *Journal of Politics* 26 (August 1964): 649-650.

21. Hollander, *Leadership Dynamics*, 7-8.

22. Lester G. Seligman, "The Study of Political Leadership," *American Political Science Review* 44 (December 1950): 915.

23. Dankwart A. Rustow, "Introduction to the Issue Philosophers and Kings: Studies in Leadership," *Daedalus* 97 (Summer 1968): 689.

24. Burns, *Leadership*, 427.

25. Donald D. Searing, "Models and Images of Man and Society in Leadership Theory," in *Political Leadership: Readings for an Emerging Field*, ed. Glenn D. Paige (New York: The Free Press, 1972), 21.

26. Ibid., 32.

27. William Fielding Ogburn, "The Great Man Versus Social Forces," *Social Forces* 5 (December 1926): 229-230.

28. For a detailed discussion of the impact of personality on society see Fred I. Greenstein, "The Impact of Personality on Politics: An Attempt to Clear Away Underbrush," *American Political Science Review* 61 (September 1967): 633-634.

29. Searing, "Models and Images," 28.

30. Quoted in Searing, "Models and Images," 33.

31. Searing, "Models and Images," 36.

32. G. Lowell Field and John Higley, *Elitism* (London: Routledge and Kegan Paul, 1980), 7.

33. Suzanne Keller, *Beyond the Ruling Class: Strategic Elites in Modern Society* (New York: Random House, 1963), 58.

34. Ibid., 25.

35. George Douglas Howard Cole, *Studies in Class Structure* (London: Routledge and Kegan Paul, 1955), 104.

36. Amitai Etzioni, *A Comparative Analysis of Complex Organizations: On Power, Involvement, and Their Correlates* (New York: The Free Press, 1961), 89.

37. Harold D. Lasswell, Daniel Lerner, and C. Easton Rothwell, *The Comparative Study of Elites: An Introduction and Bibliography* (Stanford: Stanford University Press, 1952), 13.

38. Vilfredo Pareto, *The Rise and Fall of the Elites: An Application of Theoretical Sociology*, with an introduction by Hans L. Zetterberg (Totowa, N.J.: Bedminster Press, 1968), 8.

39. Carl Joachim Friedrich, *Man and His Government: An Empirical Theory of Politics* (New York: McGraw-Hill, 1963), 316.

40. Quoted in Michalina Clifford-Vaughn, "Some French Concepts of Elites," *British Journal of Sociology* 11 (December 1960): 319.

41. See Keller, *Beyond the Ruling Class*, 9; T. B. Bottomore, *Elites and Society* (Harmondsworth, Middlesex, England: Penguin Books, 1964), 13; and Vilfredo Pareto, *Theory of Derivations*, vol. 3 of *The Mind and Society*, ed. Arthur Livingston, trans. Andrew Bongiorno and Arthur Livingston (New York: Dover Publications, 1935), 1423.

42. Keller, *Beyond the Ruling Class*, 12-13.

43. Gaetano Mosca, *The Ruling Class*, trans. Hannah D. Kahn, ed. Arthur Livingston (New York: McGraw-Hill, 1939), 50.

44. Ibid., 53

45. Renzo Sereno, "The Anti-Aristotelianism of Gaetano Mosca and Its Fate," *Ethics* 48 (1937-1938): 12.

46. Anthony Giddens, "Elites," *New Society* 22 (November 16, 1972): 390.

47. Quoted in Giddens, "Elites," 340.

48. Robert Michels, *Political Parties: A Sociological Study of the Oligarchical Tendencies of Modern Democracy*, trans. Eden Paul and Cedar Paul (New York: The Free Press, 1962), 32.

49. See: Keller, *Beyond the Ruling Class*, 14-15.

50. Ibid., 44.

51. Ibid., 65, 75, 88.

52. Carl J. Friedrich, *The New Image of the Common Man* (Boston: Beacon Press, 1950; Reprint, Westport, Conn.: Greenwood Press, 1984), 259-260.

53. Pareto, *The Rise and Fall of the Elites*, 78.

54. Field and Higley, *Elitism*, 32.

55. Ibid., 37, 92.

56. Keller, *Beyond the Ruling Class*, 273.

57. Field and Higley, *Elitism*, 19, 20.

58. Keller, *Beyond the Ruling Class*, 263.

59. Ibid., 275.

60. Ibid., 276-277.

61. Quoted in Tucker, *Politics as Leadership*, 15.

62. Ibid., 18-19.

63. Ibid., 105.

64. Keller, *Beyond the Ruling Class*, 173.

65. Ibid., 179-192. For a detailed discussion of the impact of recruitment patterns on socio-political stability and change see: Peter Bachrach, "Elite Consensus and Democracy," *Journal of Politics* 24 (August 1962): 439-452.

66. Quoted in Bottomore, *Elites and Society*, 15.

67. Mosca, *The Ruling Class*, 65.

A Framework for Analysis

68. Joseph A. Schumpeter, *Imperialism and Social Classes*, trans. Heinz Norden, ed. Paul M. Sweezy (New York: Augustus M. Kelley, 1951), 148-162.
69. Quoted in Bottomore, *Elites and Society*, 59.
70. Pareto, *The Rise and Fall of the Elites*, 9.
71. Ibid., 86. See also: Pareto, *The Mind and Society*, 3:1431.
72. Pareto, *The Rise and Fall of the Elites*, 39, 59.
73. Vilfredo Pareto, *Les Systemes Socialistes*, vol. 1 (Paris: Marcel Girard, 1926), 30.
74. Quoted in Keller, *Beyond the Ruling Class*, 243.
75. Francis Bacon, *Selected Writings of Francis Bacon* (New York: Modern Library, 1955), 36-37.
76. Quoted in Keller, *Beyond the Ruling Class*, 89.
77. Bottomore, *Elites and Society*, 15.
78. For a detailed discussion of democracy and elite plurality see: John Plamenatz and Giovanni Sartori, "Electoral Studies and Democratic Theory," *Political Studies* 6 (February 1958): 1-15.
79. Joseph A. Schumpeter, *Capitalism, Socialism, and Democracy*, 3rd ed. (New York: Harper and Bros., 1950), 285.
80. Karl Mannheim, *Ideology and Utopia: An Introduction to the Sociology of Knowledge*, trans. Louis Wirth and Edward Shils (New York: Harcourt, Brace and Co., [1936]), 119; and Karl Mannheim, *Essays on the Sociology of Culture* (London: Routledge and Paul, 1956), 179.
81. Raymond Aron, "Social Structure and the Ruling Class, Part One," *British Journal of Sociology* 1 (1950): 10.
82. Peter Bachrach, *The Theory of Democratic Elitism: A Critique* (Boston: Little, Brown and Co., 1967), 5.
83. Ibid., 37.
84. Ibid., 106.
85. Bottomore, *Elites and Society*, 126.
86. Robert A. Dahl, "Critique of the Ruling Elite Model," *American Political Science Review* 52 (June 1958): 463.
87. Glenn D. Paige, *The Scientific Study of Political Leadership*, 84.
88. Burns, *Leadership*, 243.
89. Max Weber, *The Theory of Social and Economic Organization*, trans. A. M. Henderson and Talcott Parsons (New York: Oxford University Press, 1947), 358-359.
90. For further discussion see Burns, *Leadership*, 243; K. J. Ratnam, "Charisma and Political Leadership," *Political Studies* 12 (1964): 342, 348; Paige, *The Scientific Study of Political Leadership*, 85; and Lewis A. Froman, Jr., *People and Politics* (Englewood Cliffs: Prentice-Hall, 1962), 75.
91. H. H. Gerth, "The Nazi Party: Its Leadership and Composition," *American Journal of Sociology* 45 (January 1940): 519.
92. Ratnam, "Charisma and Political Leadership," 348-349.
93. Karl Loewenstein, *Max Weber's Political Ideas in the Perspective of Our Time*, trans. Richard Winston and Clara Winston (Amherst: University of Massachusetts Press, 1966), 79.

94. Carl J. Friedrich, "Political Leadership and Charismatic Power," *Journal of Politics* 23 (February 1961): 14-16.

95. Cited in Robert C. Tucker, "The Theory of Charismatic Leadership," *Daedalus* 97 (Summer 1968): 732.

96. Quoted in Loewenstein, *Max Weber's Political Ideas*, 75.

97. Weber, *The Theory of Social and Economic Organization*, 362.

98. E. San Juan, Jr., "Orientations of Max Weber's Concept of Charisma," *The Centennial Review* 11 (Spring 1967): 277.

99. Tucker, "The Theory of Charismatic Leadership," 732-733.

100. See Burns, *Leadership*, 243.

101. For a detailed discussion of this interpretation see: Tucker, "The Theory of Charismatic Leadership," 734.

102. See George M. Kahin, Guy J. Pauker, and Lucian W. Pye, "Comparative Politics of Non-Western Countries," *American Political Science Review* 49 (December 1955): 1025.

103. Tucker, "The Theory of Charismatic Leadership," 738.

104. Richard H. Pfaff, "Petrodollars and the Legitimacy Crisis in the Middle East," in *Oil, the Middle East, North Africa and the Industrial States: Developmental and International Dimensions*, ed. Klaus Jurgen Gantzel and Helmut Mejcher (Paderborn, Germany: Ferdinand Schoningh, 1984), 256.

105. Ibid., 257.

106. Burns, *Leadership*, 246.

107. For a detailed discussion of these charismatic qualities see: Edward Shils, "The Concentration and Dispersion of Charisma: Their Bearing on Economic Policy in Underdeveloped Countries," *World Politics* 11 (October 1958-July 1959): 4; Ratnam, "Charisma and Political Leadership," 349; and Tucker, "The Theory of Charismatic Leadership," 748-749.

108. For a detailed discussion of the transformations in charismatic authority see Friedrich, *Man and His Government*, 175-179.

2

The Islamic Polity

ISLAM AND POLITICS

Islam is not simply a religion, it is a way of life. Traditionalist and reformist Sunni and Shi'i Muslims as well as non-Muslim students of Islam have accepted the universality and centrality of this belief system throughout its long history. Attempts at limiting the scope of Islam to religiosity and spirituality have been rare and unsuccessful.

Islam is universal because it governs all aspects of the believer's life. It is central in the sense that it constitutes the essential basis and focus of identity of the follower and his loyalty to the community. Membership in the Islamic community not only provides the believer with a sense of identity with a religio-political community that expands beyond ethno-national boundaries, but also instills a sense of selfhood in the believer.[1]

The Islamic doctrine of oneness (*tawhid*) is the most important element in Islamic thought. Although the doctrine explicitly refers to the oneness of God (Islamic monotheism) and His supreme sovereignty, it implicitly provides for the totality and universality of the Islamic belief system. Thus, *tawhid* is the foundation of all human activities because, as the reformist Shi'i scholar and political activist Ali Shariati observed, it integrates and unifies the followers' spirits and ultimately leads them towards a common direction.[2]

In this holistic view of life, religion is ". . . intimately and organically related to politics, law, and society," and consequently all facets of life are governed by God who is the supreme authority.[3] Since secularism as manifested in the separation of the religious realm from the political realm is neither theoretically nor practically accepted, religion and politics remain ". . . the two sides of a single coin in Islam."[4] According to Bernard Lewis,

> Islam was associated with power from the very beginning, from the first formative years of the Prophet and his immediate successors. This association between religion and power, community and polity, can already

be seen in the Qur'an itself and in the other early religious texts on which Muslims base their beliefs.[5]

This unity of religion and politics is overwhelmingly advocated by Islamic jurisprudents and political activists. The reformist and predominantly individualistic Muammar Qaddafi does not separate religion from politics because he does not see a contradiction between religious consciousness and political decisions.[6] The influential Sunni scholar Muhammad al-Ghazali, who attributed the unity of religion and politics to Islamic monotheism, rejected secularism as heresy (*bida'ah*) and favored the application of Islamic teachings to the spiritual as well as the sociopolitical lives of the believers.[7] The Shi'i traditionalist scholar and pragmatic political activist Ruhullah Khomeini emphatically rejected secularism as well. In his view, Islam is the religion of politics, and as such everything in Islam is political.[8] Khomeini paid foremost attention to the political dimension of Islam by stating that "the issues of Islam are political issues, and thus the politics of Islam gains primacy over other issues."[9] The rule of Islam is not, however, limited to political life. Islam also encompasses the material and spiritual aspects of the followers' lives from the time of birth, throughout life to death, and even after death throughout the spiritual existence.[10]

Khomeini attached unique importance to political life and believed that since Islam regulates this life "political activity is a religious responsibility"[11] of all segments of the society. Politics, from this perspective, is the followers' instrument of accepting God and obeying His will. In this sense, according to Khomeini, "Islam is a religion whose divine [spiritual] rulings are also political."[12]

To understand Khomeini's views of political life, it is critically important to be familiar with his conception of politics. Central to this conception is leadership of the community. Khomeini observed that ". . . politics means running the state."[13] Running the state involves ". . . a relationship between the governor and the people, between governments and masses, between the governors and other governments; and the prevention of corruption."[14] Khomeini's typology of politics includes Satanic politics, which is based on corrupt leadership, unjust rule over people and their properties, and lies; and Islamic politics that guides the society towards all individual and societal needs.[15]

The identification of these needs is not left to the community, rather it is the leadership's responsibility to determine what the desired goals are, and to lead the community towards them. Shariati believed that the goal of politics is not so much the attainment of all individual rights and needs in the society, as it is the identification of these needs and rights and the education of the people to accept them.[16]

These views are not confined solely to Shi'ism but have widespread support within the Sunni scholarship as well. Shaykh Mahmud Shaltut, the influential revivalist Abul A'la Mawdudi and his disciple Sayyid Qutb and a host of other classic and contemporary, reformist and traditionalist Sunni scholars have advocated the universality of Islam. Mawdudi believed that the Islamic legal code (*Shari'ah*) justifies universality because this code does not distinguish between religion and other aspects of life, particularly between religion and politics.[17] He insisted that there is no area of man's activity and concern to which the *Shari'ah* does not address itself with specific divine guidance.

Mawdudi equated secularism with religionlessness (*la-din*), which is considered contrary to Islam. Hence, secularism is shunned because it could conceivably exclude all morality, ethics or human decency from the controlling mechanisms of society. Morality of any kind is simply inconceivable without religion and the sanction of eternal punishment to support it, Mawdudi concluded. In his view, "when religion is relegated to the personal realm, men inevitably give way to their bestial impulses and perpetrate evil upon one another. In fact, it is precisely because they wish to escape the restraints of morality and the divine guidance that men espouse secularism."[18] Consequently, in this context Islamic universalism is salvation in this and the next worlds.

Secularism distinguishes the ignorant (*jahili*) culture, according to Qutb. In his typology of cultures, Qutb referred to an Islamic culture that is based on the fundamentals of the Islamic world view, and a *jahili* culture which ". . . manifests itself in a variety of systems, all of which can be explained by one principle . . . that of elevating human thought [to the status] of a God not necessitating recourse to God's guidance."[19] The *jahili* culture is, therefore, only subservient to its own rules and obedient to its own visions, values, concepts, traditions and customs. Disregard for God's guidance is the product of human ignorance, weakness and desire that fail to provide solutions to human problems and that inevitably result in harm to some segments of society.[20] To establish a dynamic and integrated Islamic system with superior strategy and ideology under God's command, secularism should be eradicated.[21]

Advocates of secularism in Islam have based their arguments on juridical/theoretical and historical foundations. However, many of these arguments rely on narrow and somewhat misleading interpretations of the Quranic rulings and the history of Islam. For example, Ali 'Abd al-Raziq and Chiragh 'Ali define politics as exclusively man's rational task that has nothing to do with religion. Al-Raziq argues that in Islam religion and politics are separate because the Quran did not provide specific political instructions, and Muhammad's tradition (*Sunnah*) clearly shows that his authority over the community had nothing to do with temporal power and was simply a religious mission. The dissonance within the community that immediately developed after Muhammad, and the emergence of the institutions of *khalifah* and *imamah* were purely of a political nature and had little to do with religion. The *khalifah* system ". . . has nothing in common with religious functions, no more than the judiciary and the other essential functions and machinery of power and state," al-Raziq concludes.[22] Politics, he observes, is simply left to the believers who will have recourse to rational judgement and base their decisions on experience and rules of politics. Only selfish leaders in pursuit of their own interests committed the crime of mixing Islam with politics in the name of religion, al-Raziq suggests.

These secularist interpretations do not reflect the spirit of the Quran nor the historical experiences of Muslim societies. The Quran's lack of specific references to political principles, the specificity that al-Raziq and Chiragh 'Ali deem necessary, does not mean that Islam accepts secularism. Lack of specificity was mostly intended to keep the Quran a universal book applicable to all people at all times, and thus to preserve the adaptability and vitality of Islam. While the Quran and other Islamic sources explicitly affirm the totality and universality of Islam, there is no reason to believe that politics was intended to be excluded. Clearly, Muhammad's right to temporal authority has been recognized even by the Shi'is who have questioned the legitimacy (*haqqaniyyah*) of the *khalifah* system. Accordingly, he and his successors did exercise their right to temporal power.

However, to conclude that Islamic societies have not experienced secularist tendencies is to paint an inaccurate picture of their contemporary history. As in the Christian world, Muslim societies have in varying degrees experienced separation of religion and politics. The current Islamic revivalist movement is partly a response to the goals and policy implications of secularism and nationalism of the twentieth century in the Muslim world.

THE ISLAMIC STATE

Foundations

The idea of an Islamic state is as old as Islam itself. Muslims' widespread and forceful attempts to establish an Islamic state have been explained by communal needs, Islamic universalism, explicit Quranic instructions and the prophet's tradition.

With the emergence of an Islamic community (*ummah*) and its expansion beyond ethno-national boundaries, the need for an Islamic state which governs on the basis of Islamic principles arises. As Manzooruddin

Ahmed observes, "once the moral and psychological foundations of the *ummah* are laid on the basis of a primordial convenant [sic], the next stage in the development of the *ummah* leads to the emergence of organized authority."[23] Historically speaking, during the formative years of the *ummah*, political authority was not organized; thus, Ahmed argues, the prophet functioned as a substitute for this authority. However, with the expansion of Islam and the subsequent sectarian trends in the community after Muhammad, the need for authority in the form of an Islamic state was recognized and intensely pursued by the community.

The universality of Islam also warrants the establishment of an Islamic state because the state is a necessary instrument for the implementation of divinely-ordained Islamic principles that are to govern all aspects of the believers' lives. According to Mawdudi, the realization of the objectives of the *Shari'ah* is simply impossible without the agency of the state and the power it commands. In his view,

> . . . the reforms which Islam wants to bring about cannot be carried out merely by sermons. Political power is essential for their achievement . . . the struggle for obtaining control over the organs of the state when motivated by the urge to establish the *din* [religion] and the Islamic *Shari'ah* and to enforce the Islamic injunctions, is not only permissible but is positively desirable and as such obligatory.[24]

Ideally, an Islamic state provides a framework for the life of the individual believer and the community as a whole by playing an essential role in the perpetuation of Islamic law and in the maintenance of social order. Khomeini observed that in the absence of this state ". . . one can expect anarchy."[25] Shariati, however, distinguished between an institution and a movement by stressing that the former is inert while the latter is dynamic.[26] He criticized the establishment of an Islamic state—an institution—for its conduciveness to inertness and favored a dynamic Islamic order. Ironically, Shariati never made a precise and practical distinction between the Islamic order and the Islamic state, and did not acknowledge that the Islamic order—which he cherished so dearly—was also designed to institutionalize Islamic principles and, thus, was subject to inertness. Obviously, Shariati's dislike for an institutionalized Islamic state was due to his fear of a state that ". . . would institutionalize the power of a clerical profession and find justifications for traditional folk practices used to subordinate the masses to that power."[27] The transformation of Alid Shi'ism, which was a dynamic movement, into the inert institution of Safavid Shi'ism attests to the danger of this type of institutionalization, according to Shariati.[28]

An Alternative State

The Islamic state is distinct from other types of states by its unique theoretical foundations and structural as well as functional features. A state is not Islamic simply because it is inhabited predominantly or even entirely by Muslims, but rather, as Muhammad Asad points out, it is Islamic ". . . by virtue of a conscious application of the sociopolitical tenets of Islam to the life of the nation, and by an incorporation of those tenets in the basic constitution of the country."[29] Therefore, Western labels of democracy, authoritarianism, socialism, etc., are not proper means of identification if applied to the Islamic state. The Islamic state, as an ideological state, ". . . has a social orientation peculiar to itself, different in many respects from that of the modern West, and can be successfully interpreted only within its own context and in its own terminology."[30] As discussed in the following pages, one might compare certain Islamic thoughts and practices to non-Islamic ones. However, it is inappropriate to label the Islamic state as "democratic," "authoritarian," "socialistic," etc., without recognizing what democracy, authoritarianism, socialism, etc., mean in the context of Islamic thought.

The Islamic state is not democratic, in the Western sense of the term, because Islam rejects the notion of popular sovereignty, and, by recognizing the sovereignty of God, makes it incumbent upon the followers to follow His lead by complying with the *Shari'ah* instructions. Submission to God's sovereignty undoubtedly imposes restrictions upon individual and communal rights that are the fundamental attributes of popular sovereignty and an integral component of the Western conception of democracy. It is argued, however, that such restrictions on rights do not necessarily make the Islamic state authoritarian, because under the supervision of and in compliance with the *Shari'ah* the community still maintains broad discretion in decision-making. As Asad observes,

> Being a Divine Ordinance, it [*Shari'ah*] duly anticipates the fact of historical evolution, and confronts the believer with no more than a very limited number of broad political principles; beyond that, it leaves a vast field of constitution-making activity, of governmental methods, and of day-to-day legislation to the *ijtihad* [independent judgement] of the time concerned.[31]

This view has not convinced many Islamic scholars of the democratic nature of the Islamic state. Some have argued that ". . . Islam is, as far as political philosophy is concerned, the very antithesis of Western democratic principles."[32] Abu Nasr al-Farabi and ibn-Rushd, whose writings and thoughts were influenced by Platonic thought, rejected the claim that the Islamic doctrine of communal consent (*ijma*), even in its original definition that was a reference to the consent of the community at large, is able to guarantee democratic values in the Islamic state.[33]

Khomeini believed that the Islamic state is democratic. However, he stressed that unlike the corrupt Western and Eastern democracies,[34] the Islamic democracy is the rightful democracy because it guarantees the true liberty of the community. His understanding of Islamic democracy entails the Islamic notions of liberty and equality. Islamic liberty, unlike the Western notion of liberty, is defined by Islamic laws and consists of the liberties that have been provided by God. According to Khomeini, the liberties that God has given us are the logical liberties.[35] Islamic equality that is a component of Islamic democracy is also defined by Islamic laws and primarily refers to the social rather than the politico-economic equality of the believers. Muhammad Iqbal praised Islamic democracy for being based on equality, and criticized Western democracy for being ". . . a system where people are counted but not weighed."[36]

Opposition to Western style democracy is not only explained by the principle of God's sovereignty, but also by the realities and necessities of the politics of traditional societies. Shariati rejected the idea of popular sovereignty because, in his opinion, in the backward nations people are not in a position to identify and pursue the course of action that is best for them. Moreover, democracy is incompatible with the goal of traditional societies to advance because democracy is inclined to preserve the status quo.[37] Therefore, he believed the Islamic state has to avoid democracy in order to maintain its dynamism.

This does not, however, mean that Islam has never ruled on the basis of communal consent (*ijma*). Apparently, even some Shi'is, who reserve God the sovereign rights and supreme authority, believe that the choice of the leadership is the right of the community during the occultation of the twelfth imam of Shi'ism, Mahdi. In their view, the Islamic state during this period is democratic because the "power of sovereignty derives from the *ummah*."[38]

Historically, the Arab traditional institution of *al-Nadawa*, whereby communal affairs were run by mutual consultation among tribal elders, became an instrument of democracy in Sunni Islam and contributed to the Quranic institution of consultation (*shura*). This Quranic instrument ". . . clearly establishes that the Islamic State derives its sanction from the Islamic community and that, therefore, it is completely democratic."[39] This does not mean that the Islamic community is sovereign. As Mawdudi observed, the ultimate sovereignty rests in God.[40] Therefore, all communal decisions should correspond to God's will, as illustrated in the Quran, and to Muhammad's *Sunnah*.

The scope and even the legitimacy (*haqqaniyyah*) of *shura* has been particularly questioned by the Shi'is. Even the orthodox Sunni institution of communal consensus was redefined by Shi'ism to refer to the consensus of the clergy (ulama) rather than the community at large. Therefore, in the Shi'i thought, neither of these institutions are the instruments of democracy. In fact, the Shi'i idea of the clerics' consensus (*ijma*) is conducive to elitism rather than democracy. While many scholars do not question the need for experts in Islamic law, they reject this type of elitism because ". . . even after the experts' advice, the final decision remains with the community and its representatives in the legislature."[41]

The Islamic alternative state is necessitated by the inadequacies of both democratic and socialist states. Qutb, a disciple of Mawdudi and an influential revivalist, criticized democracy and capitalism by asking:

> Who will dare to claim that those million of hungry, naked, barefoot peasants whose intestines are devoured by worms, whose eyes are bitten by flies and whose blood is sucked by insects are humans who enjoy human dignity and human rights [as the Capitalist slogans claim?]. . . . Who will dare to claim that the hundreds of thousands of disabled beggars, who search for crumbs in garbage boxes, who are naked, barefoot, with faces crusted with dirt. . . . Who will dare to say that they are the source of authority in the nation, based on democratic election?[42]

He also rejected socialism for its preoccupation with materialism, and claimed that "communism in itself is an insignificant idea which deserves no respect from those who think humanely, above the level of food and drink."[43] Peoples' attraction to communism, Qutb observed, stems from their experience with, and dislike for, the evils of capitalism. The Islamic state offers an alternative to both democratic and socialist states, and assists in solving the problems that have made socialism such an appealing alternative to capitalism.[44]

The Islamic state, which is founded upon Islamic principles rather than alien ideas and represents contemporary needs of the Islamic community, frees Muslims from subservience to alien values; provides them with social justice, international respect and dignity; and protects them against the evils of strife and war. According to Qutb, the Islamic alternative is "a system that provides us with the bread that communism provides, and frees us from economic and social disparity, realizing a balanced society while sustaining us spiritually."[45]

Since the Islamic state is founded upon the Islamic vision and communal needs, as long as these needs correspond with the vision, it maintains some dynamism and ". . . is not restricted solely to a replica of the first Islamic society, but is every social form governed by the total Islamic view of life. . . ." This state, then, ". . . has room for scores of models which are compatible with the natural growth of a society and the new needs of the contemporary age as long as the total Islamic idea dominates these models in its expansive external perimeter."[46] Qutb sums up the fundamental features of the Islamic vision by arguing that it is unique, comprehensive, constant, monolithic, balanced, positive and pragmatic.

The uniqueness of this vision is attributed to its divine source, which distinguishes it from other systems of thought that are responses to local and temporary needs of communities.[47] This divine origin also guarantees the Islamic vision's originality, comprehensiveness and applicability to the modern world, according to Qutb. Other systems of thought derive from human whims and desires and thus they can never be comprehensive and remain intact. In Qutb's view, "it is impossible that a human concept or a humanly devised system would ever personify comprehensiveness. It will be temporary or fragmentary."[48] By relying on the Quran, Qutb claimed that it is "Islam alone [that] has remained preserved in its principles. Its sources have not been polluted, nor has its truth been superimposed with falsehood."

Although the Islamic vision is comprehensive (*shumul*), human abilities are limited in comprehending its totality. According to Qutb, man ". . . is limited by his creaturehood. . . . He is not perfect or eternal. His ability to know is limited by his nature and function, which is vicegerency on the earth through which the meaning of worship is fulfilled. He has been granted the capacity to comprehend what is necessary for his role as vicegerent, no less, no more." The comprehensiveness, precision, depth and authenticity of this vision reject any need for foreign principles to complement it. God, according to Qutb, has sent this vision ". . . in all its particularities and its essentials. It is received by 'man' in its perfect condition. He is not to complement it from his own [resources] or delete any of it; rather he is to appropriate it and implement all its essentials in his life."[49]

The constancy (*thabat*) in these essentials also results from the overriding principle of God's supremacy (*rabbaniyyah*). This constancy, according to Qutb, provides for a dynamism within a constant set of perimeters rather than the ossification of life and thought.[50] This dynamism which allows for the implementation of the Islamic ideology in different forms of society rejects unrestricted values, thoughts and progress. Instead, constancy in the essentials assures the order of society and universe as well as the harmony and integration of Muslim life within this order. This gives progressive direction to the followers' actions, ". . . as willed by God, linking yesterday, today and tomorrow."[51]

The unity of the Islamic vision proceeding from Islamic monotheism (*tawhid*) manifests itself in the areas of ". . . thought and behavior, vision and initiative, doctrine and system, source and reception, life and death, striving and movement, life and means of livelihood, this world and the next. It does not divide into sections, seek various paths or horizons or march on different roads without agreement."[52] This monolithicism of thought and action that originates from God's ultimate and uncontested supreme will, as expressed in the *Shari'ah* and other Islamic sources, rejects any form of factionalism in the Islamic state.

Unique to Islam is a harmony or balance (*tawazun*) that can be established between what is revealed, and what humans can grasp, and what is accepted only through faith. This balance between the known and the unknown, the revealed and the hidden, is compatible with the human nature that recognizes God's absolute knowledge and trusts Him. This relationship of obedience to God by the creature is founded on a sense of certainty and positiveness (*ijabiyyah*) that guide the followers' actions and govern their affairs.

The Islamic vision is also pragmatic (*waqiiyyah*) because while it aspires to the ideal goal of establishing the highest and most perfect system, it is grounded in the reality of life and seeks a system to which humanity can ascend.

Characteristics

The ideal Islamic state is a constitutional state founded upon the basic principles of the Islamic vision, and as such it is distinct from other types of states in terms of its philosophical foundations, structural as well as functional features and policy decisions.

The Political System

The constitution of the Islamic state derives from the *Shari'ah* whose authority is explicitly asserted in the Quran and by the prophet's tradition. The Quran upholds that ". . . the authority rests with none but Allah [God]. He has commanded you to worship none save Him. This is the right way of life . . ."[53] This authority that is expressed in the *Shari'ah* is total and exclusive because the Quran maintains, ". . . Say (O Muhammad): The authority belongs to Allah alone."[54] In reference to Muhammad's prophecy, the Quran acknowledges that "We sent no messenger save that he should be obeyed by Allah's command."[55] Muhammad confessed that ". . . I do not follow anything except what is revealed to me [by Allah],"[56] and obeyed God's supreme will throughout his life.

Despite the consensus on the authority of the *Shari'ah*, no general agreement exists on its sources and their relative significance. These disagreements are both sectarian and juridical. According to Mawdudi, the principal sources of the *Shari'ah* are the Quran, the *Sunnah* of the prophet, the conventions and practices of the four Rightly-Guided Caliphs and the opinions of the great Islamic jurists.[57] The importance and primacy of the Quran and Muhammad's *Sunnah* are predominantly attested to, as long as the validity of the prophet's *Sunnah* is not in doubt. However, the legitimacy of other sources and their relative importance are questioned by various schools of jurisprudence. Some sects, particularly Shi'ism, have also relied on the sayings of the prophet (*Hadith*) and of the Shi'i imams (*Ravayah*) as the other major sources of the *Shari'ah*.

Unlike man-made laws that are inadequate and incomplete, the *Shari'ah* is an organic and integrated set of rules that comprehensively governs every aspect of the followers' lives. Everything that Muslims enact or observe in their societies should be measured against the dictates and the spirit of the *Shari'ah*. According to Mawdudi, the *Shari'ah* touches upon such matters as:

> religious rituals, personal character, morals, habits, family relationships, social and economic affairs, administration, rights, and duties of citizens, judicial system, laws of war and peace and international relations. . . . The *Shariah* is a complete scheme of life and an all-embracing social order where nothing is superfluous and nothing is lacking.[58]

As the constitution of the state, the *Shari'ah* generally recognizes the three principles of right, justice and equality of all Muslims regardless of their ethno-national and racial distinctions. Although the *Shari'ah* designates the boundaries of individual and communal rights, it clearly defines liberty in terms of submission to God by requiring Muslims to abide by His will as expressed in the *Shari'ah*, if Muslims seek earthly blessings and heavenly rewards. Mawdudi asserted that refusal to submit to these ordained rules produces evil, unhappiness and eternal punishment for the followers.

This exclusive authority of the *Shari'ah* reaffirms the sovereignty of God, repudiates the doctrine of popular sovereignty and founds the Islamic state upon the doctrine of God's sovereignty and the vicegerency of man. Man's vicegerency guarantees him certain liberties under the suzerainty of God. Therefore, in the Islamic state which is the "kingdom of God," because God is its ultimate sovereign, Mawdudi concluded, followers are free to make decisions within the confines of the *Shari'ah* and in compliance with the spirit of God's will.

The *Shari'ah* specifically recognizes the authority of the doctrine of *shura* for arriving at communal decisions, but it is not specific and clear about the authority of the doctrine of *ijma*. It is clear, however, that "every Muslim who is capable and qualified to give a sound opinion on matters of Islamic law, is entitled to interpret the law of God when such interpretation becomes necessary."[59]

In view of the limitations on popular sovereignty, the Islamic political system is monolithic rather than pluralistic. This monolithicism that apparently rules out any genuine debate on basic matters is the result of the totality of the Islamic vision consisting of a vast and integrated system of ideas that must be realized in their entirety. Any genuine Islamic position has to be accepted by the community, with no possibility of disagreement. Khomeini asserted that any opposition to and disagreement about the Islamic republic is treason. He rejected sectarian disagreements and any practices and views which oppose the Islamic institutions and views, no matter whether these views belong to individuals, groups or parties.[60]

Khomeini even justified Islamic monolithicism on practical grounds by arguing that ". . . all groups should merge into one group, that being an Islamic group"[61] because "the establishment of various groups is a deadly poison for the nation."[62] As to political parties, he declared that "all factions should become one and develop into a united front. One front, one party, the party of God (*Hizb Allah*)."[63]

According to Khomeini, monolithicism does not make the Islamic system dictatorial because the Islamic system is a constitutional system founded upon the conditions underlined by the *Shari'ah*. In this sense, he observed, the Islamic constitutional system is democratic.[64]

The *Shari'ah* has not specified the structural and functional features of the political system. Therefore, it has been concluded that ". . . the Muslim community is free to evolve any suitable method for the enforcement of Islamic law,"[65] as long as these methods comply with the general *Shari'ah* instructions. In view of the overriding principles of Islamic totality and monolithicism, then, the Islamic government should be based on the doctrine of fusion of powers rather than a radical separation of powers.

The Islamic doctrine of fusion of powers which ". . . constitutes a most important, specifically Islamic contribution to political theory," provides for Islamic unity, reinforces the monolithic nature of the Islamic government and prevents constant conflicts among various branches of government that make Western democratic pluralist systems ineffective.[66] As far as governmental structures and functions are concerned, fusion of powers requires overlapping executive, legislative and judicial branches that perform mostly shared functions.

As in traditional polities, where patrimonialism is the rule and political institutions are either non-existent or underdeveloped and ineffective, branches of the Islamic government are basically non-institutionalized. Most discussions about the executive branch focus on the head of state, the leadership, rather than an elaborate set of structures that are primarily involved in the execution of policies. This feature signifies the role of leadership in the Islamic and other traditional polities. In the Islamic state, the leader who is the head of state exercises superior power at the helm of a hierarchy which designates to him a position above the other two branches. This position makes the leader the primary subject and the ultimate executor of the *Shari'ah*. Islamic political leadership is extensively studied in the ensuing chapters.

Due to the comprehensive nature of the *Shari'ah*, establishment of a truly functional legislative branch is not generally deemed necessary. Khomeini believed that what is needed is a planning council (*Majlis-i barnameh rizi*), rather than a legislative council, to make plans for executive agencies to facilitate their efficient performance.[67] A true legislative body is not necessary, Khomeini asserted, because unlike democratic systems in which representatives legislate, in the Islamic government ". . . God alone is the ruler and the legislator."[68] However, a consultative body is necessary to conduct consultation among Muslims in dealing with their affairs, as required by the doctrine of *shura*, and to enable the community to find laws rather than make them. It is these functions that make this body a consultative council (*Majlis-i shura*) rather than a legislative one.

Although Islam has not specified any method for the choice of deputies to this council, the same considerations that apply to the choice of the leader govern their recruitment. Thus, at least from the Sunni perspective, it is the right and responsibility of the people to determine through mutual consultation who should be a member of this body. Ironically, these individuals were not recruited to the office through election during the four Rightly-Guided Caliphs. This choice was, however, the result of the circumstances of the time rather than a flat rejection of the method of election for recruiting members to this council.[69]

Of primary importance is the qualities of individuals rather than the methods by which they are recruited to the position. The recruitment process ". . . should result in the choice of the best people by whatever means that result may be achieved."[70] Like the leader, deputies to this council must be adult males who are trustworthy, knowledgeable about and observant of the *Shari'ah*. This requires a working knowledge of Arabic in order to understand the Quran and to derive the authentic *Sunnah* from other Islamic texts; and an insight into the specific injunctions of the *Shari'ah* and opinions of experts (*mujtahidin*) in previous generations. These deputies' knowledge of Islam should, however, be balanced by their solid understanding of the contemporary issues. Mawdudi emphasized that the most fundamental of all these qualifications is these deputies' superior character and record of good conduct, for corrupt individuals will not inspire people and will not secure their observance of laws.

This council's major functions entail consulting the leader and finding laws stipulated by the *Shari'ah* rather than making them. However, these limitations do not exclude the council from limited legislative functions. As Mawdudi observed,

> ... One is apt to think these fundamental facts [i.e., God's sovereignty and the necessity of obedience to the prophet's *Sunnah*] leave no room for human legislation in an Islamic state, because herein all legislative functions vest in God and the only function left for Muslims lies in their observance of the God-made law vouchsafed to them through the agency of the prophet. The fact of the matter, however, is that Islam does not totally exclude human legislation. It only limits its scope and guides it on right lines.[71]

The law-finding function, in Mawdudi's view, is carried out by the means of interpretation, analogy (*qiyas*) and inference. The need for the interpretation of the *Shari'ah* arises out of the generality of its injunctions. Whenever the council engages in a search for the precise nature, scope, intent, specifics and applicability of the law it is in reality engaging in law-finding. Also, when the *Shari'ah* has not laid down specific injunctions but has made provisions for analogous situations in which similar principles are applicable, it is the council's responsibility to determine what those situations are. Most Sunni Muslims who follow the opinion of the great Sunni jurist al-Shafii recognize *qiyas* as one of the main sources of the Islamic law. Moreover, when the *Shari'ah* speaks in generalities and provides nothing specific, the council's responsibility is to infer from general principles to derive guidance for specific situations. In performing this function, the council should realize God's intent and the *Shari'ah*'s spirit, and should formulate specific injunctions accordingly.

The council is also involved in actual legislation since ". . . there is yet another vast range of human affairs about which the *Shari'ah* is totally silent."[72] Mawdudi asserted that where God has said nothing, He has left it to the discretion and judgement of men to make the laws which they see fit. Human discretion and judgement should, however, comply with the spirit and principles of Islam.

As a consultative body, the council is at the disposal of the leader for him to consult. However, in the monolithic Islamic system where the leader enjoys a unique and superior position of authority, the council's opinions are not binding either on the leader or the general public. Thus, according to Mawdudi, so long as the leader is right, complete authority remains with him and he may disregard the legislature's opinions. Theoretically speaking, the primacy of the leader's authority along with ideological monolithicism in Islam bring about a conflict-free relationship between the executive and the legislature in the Islamic government.[73]

The judiciary, functionally an independent arm of the Islamic government, is needed, Khomeini asserted, ". . . in order to maintain Islamic laws and perpetuate the essence of law, it is essential that an Islamic government has a judicial arm as prescribed by the *Shariah*. It will, together with the executive, protect Islam against anarchy and abuse."[74]

The judiciary upholds the *Shari'ah* through interpretation of and adjudication in accordance with this law. The scope of its adjudicative function is so broad as to cover conflicts among Muslims as well as between Muslims and their leaders.

The Economic System

The Quran does not specify the characteristics of the Islamic system, because it is logically impossible for this book to remain ". . . a Universal Book of Guidance, available to all people and valid for all times,"[75] if it lays down specific injunctions. Therefore, the Islamic community is free to exercise some degree of flexibility in the choice of its social, economic and political systems. However, no system can be established that does not conform to the three *Shari'ah* principles of justice, right and equality.

The Islamic economic system should at least conform to the two principles of justice and individual and communal rights.[76] The prophet advocated the establishment of a just Islamic order and is believed to have said: "My Lord enjoys justice."[77] Khomeini claimed that "all Islamic principles are just" and therefore "no regime is more just for the people than the Islamic regime."[78] He affirmed that the Islamic Republic means a just Islamic rule. It is Islam's clear mandate, A. K. Brohi observes, to ". . . establish a just order—whether that has reference to economic, political or social order in the community."[79]

Economic justice in Islam requires a redistribution of wealth and income, but it does not intend to reward everyone equally irrespective of their contributions to society. Actually, Islam tolerates some economic inequality because people are not perceived to be equal in their character, ability and service to society.[80]

Individual and communal rights and responsibilities are also inalienable components of the Islamic economic system. However, unlike capitalism, in Islam social justice takes precedence over individual rights. Therefore, individual rights are protected only to the extent that they conform to the overall social needs. For instance, Islam recognizes the individual right to private property as long as this right does not interfere with communal needs and goals.

Private ownership of property is not absolute in Islam because, as indicated in the doctrine of oneness (*tawhid*), absolute ownership belongs to God alone. According to Abul Hasan Bani-Sadr, the first president of the Islamic Republic of Iran, "absolute ownership is God's alone; to reflect the principle of *tawhid*, human ownership must be relative only."[81] Furthermore, this relative ownership is limited to constructive purposes for the benefit of the community. Any individual ownership which does not pursue the good of the community is prohibited in Islam. The right to ownership is also limited to the items that are the products of one's labor. Therefore, Islam does not acknowledge the individual right to ownership of natural resources, since natural resources are not the products of an individual's labor.

In the event that individual and communal rights and needs are incompatible, the Islamic state gives primacy to the communal rights and needs by restricting individual rights. However, these restrictions ". . . are compatible with human nature and with an equitable system and with the rights of all participants [in the society]."[82] When individual and communal needs are in harmony, individual rights should be respected, and a delicate balance between the two should be established. Bani-Sadr asserts that in all circumstances, the communal rights and needs are foremost. According to him, the community is the primary vicegerent of God and therefore its rights should gain precedence over the rights of individuals whose ownership of their labor are dependent upon the primacy of communal ownership.[83]

Unlike the capitalist law of supply and demand which defines demand as the ability to buy regardless of need, the Islamic economic system only recognizes those demands that arise out of necessity. According to Mahmud Taliqani, in the Islamic system ". . . supply and the actual making available of goods will be limited to what is actually required by necessity."[84] It is inconsistent with the Islamic notions of right, social justice and social responsibility to create a marketplace based on false demand and oppressive profits.

The economic responsibilities of individual Muslims are designed to establish justice in the Islamic society. The Quran explicitly expresses the importance of these responsibilities when it obliges every individual Muslim to participate in economically productive activities.[85] Qutb stated that "Islam is the enemy of idleness in the name of worship and religion. Worship is not an occupation of life. It has but its appointed time. . . ."[86] According to the Quran, Muslims who are expected to work hard are entitled to a share of what they earn. They are not, however, allowed to withhold all their earnings, nor are they permitted to use these earnings in a manner or in the categories prohibited by God. Thus, the use of earnings for wanton public display is prohibited. Any attempt to block the use of wealth carries severe chastisement because it causes oppression and upsets social balance.[87]

The Quran explicitly dictates the communal responsibilities of individual followers. In order to establish a just order, it is the responsibility of every individual Muslim to provide for the welfare of other members of the community. This requires that individual Muslims produce more than their own needs in order to participate in the process of purification of their wealth by providing security for others through alms tax (*zakat*)— a tax on the net wealth of the individual Muslim rather than his income. Furthermore, economic justice necessitates the prohibition of individuals from engaging in such economic activities as usury (*riba*), gambling, deceit, hoarding and monopolizing resources.

As a welfare state, the Islamic state is charged with a similar responsibility towards the community. Muhammad reaffirmed this responsibility by declaring, "He whom God has made an administrator over the affairs of Muslims but remains indifferent to their needs and their poverty, God will also be indifferent to his needs and poverty." He also said, "He who leaves behind him dependents, they are our responsibility," and observed that "the ruler [state] is the supporter of him who has no supporter."[88] To carry out these responsibilities that aim at restoring a sense of community among believers, the state relies on revenues from *zakat*, natural resources, borrowing and the sale of relevant services.

A major area of contention among students of Islam is the comparison between the Islamic economic system and capitalism, on the one hand, and socialism, on the other. The Islamic economic system that is based upon Islamic laws and morality cannot be totally identified with one or the other because it is unique in nature, even though there are similarities between the Islamic economic system and both capitalism and socialism. As Brohi observes, identifying the Islamic economic system with either of these contending systems ". . . to the exclusion of others, is sacrilegious and indeed the making of such a claim betrays a grave misunderstanding of the import and significance of the teachings of our Prophet."[89]

Unlike capitalism and socialism which are mainly preoccupied with materialism and have no regard for the spiritual, Islam considers materialism but underscores spirituality and morality, and interprets society and history in non-material terms. According to Mustafa Mahmud, "sincere, upright action before God is both material and spiritual."[90] Furthermore, while the Islamic economic system respects equality and freedom in the pursuit of a just order, Brohi claims, ". . . Socialism pursues equality and deprives us of our freedom and Capitalism pursues ideals of freedom, but deprives us of our right to equality."[91] Therefore, capitalism and socialism are *unjust orders*.

To think of the Islamic economic system as a socialistic system—an idea that has gained unprecedented popularity—is to assume ". . . that Islamic values and primacy of economic value can at all co-exist."[92] Islam's demand for total allegiance and submission from its followers requires all Muslims to give up values, economic and otherwise, for the sake of God. This clearly puts Islam in contradiction with the primacy of economic values. Furthermore, the notion of Islamic socialism, Brohi concludes, inappropriately spiritualizes socialism that is merely founded upon materialism which is alien to Islamic spiritual principles.[93]

The irrelevancy of capitalism and socialism to today's Islamic societies is not only explained by philosophical and socio-political reasons, but also by,

> . . . a host of more mundane and economic reasons, like differences in relative resource bases, changed international economic situations, benchmark differences in the levels of the respective economies, socio-economic costs of development, and above all, for the fundamental fact that the crucial developmental strategy of both the systems—industrialisation primarily through maximisation of investible surplus—is not suited to the conditions of the Muslim world and the demands of the Islamic social ideals.[94]

Contrary to these criticisms and the radical rejection of both capitalism and socialism, the Islamic welfare-state system bears important similarities to both. On the one hand, the Islamic economic system embraces the basic pursuits of capitalism that includes profit making through economic activity and basic rights to private property. On the other hand, it advocates the socialistic principle of the primacy of communal rights and justice over individual rights.

The Social System

As in the Islamic political and economic systems, the interrelated principles of right, justice and equality are the foundations of the Islamic social system. In view of these principles, the Islamic state is charged with the responsibility of protecting the rights of the citizens and of creating an egalitarian society. According to Qutb, the principle of equity governs every aspect of life in an Islamic state.[95]

Membership in the Islamic society requires the acceptance of Islamic values rather than ethno-national and racial characteristics. Mawdudi astutely emphasized this ideological harmony of the believers and observed that, "All those persons who . . . surrender themselves to the will of God are welded into a community and that is how the 'Muslim society' comes into being. Thus, this is an ideological society—a society radically different from those which spring from accidents of race, color, or country."[96]

Therefore, what distinguishes individuals in this diverse Islamic society is their acceptance, or lack of acceptance, of Islam. Those who accept Islam and observe its rulings are collectively considered to be the vicegerents of God, and as such they are equal with each other. According to Khomeini, "In Islam, there is no distinction between the rich and the poor, between black and white, between Shi'i and Sunni, between Arab and non-Arab, between Turks and non-Turks." Thus, Khomeini observed, all segments of the society are guaranteed liberty,[97] and ". . . races, groups, factions, and things of this sort do not have any primacy [over one another]. Islam is for everyone, and in everyone's benefit."[98] Shaykh Muhammad Husayn Na'ini, a noted Shi'i scholar, is also of the opinion that, "The law of equality is among the most noble of the blessed derived laws of Islamic polity. It is the basis and foundation of justice and the spirit of all the laws. . . . The essence of the holy law consists in this."[99]

Not all Muslims are equal however. The superiority of some Muslims over others is due to personal abilities and characters. Islam judges the individual by the performance of his social obligations, and ". . . does not seek to establish social justice by steam-rolling all into a state of unmerited equality."[100]

A fundamental implication of the ideological character of the Islamic state is an explicit distinction between Muslims and non-Muslim citizens of the Islamic state with regard to socio-economic and political rights and responsibilities. Muslim scholars have argued that since the foundation of the Islamic society is based on the ideology of Islam, it is logical to conclude that the citizen's status should be determined on the basis of his commitment to the ideology, a criterion that clearly assigns unequal status to Muslims and non-Muslims. Therefore, Islam designates two types of citizenship: first class citizenship to Muslims, and second-class citizenship to non-Muslims who have agreed to be loyal and obedient to the Islamic state in which they reside.

According to Mawdudi, Muslims should be reserved full rights, and consequently should assume full responsibility in managing the affairs of the state because they alone fully believe in it.[101] In his view, Muslims should have exclusive right to positions of authority, since it is illogical to expect non-Muslim citizens (*zimmis* or *dhimmis*) to uphold Islamic principles. He observed, "It is a dictate of this very nature of the Islamic state that such a state should be run only by those who believe in the ideology on which it is based and in the Divine Law which it is assigned to administer."[102] Being a Muslim is a requirement but certainly not the only qualification for the leader of the state. In addition to being Muslims, leaders should know Islamic law and its spirit and should devote themselves to its observance and enforcement.

While non-Muslim citizens are guaranteed such rights as physical protection, property ownership and preservation of their culture and religion, they are neither entitled to the right of full political expression nor are they guaranteed full equality with their fellow Muslim citizens. Although Mawdudi favored the inclusion of non-Muslims in the Islamic state, he rigorously opposed their appointment to positions that influence policy decisions. To ensure the dominance of Muslims, he suggested, non-Muslims should be excluded from the electoral process.[103] Historically speaking, non-Muslim citizens of the Islamic state have generally been excluded from sensitive positions of authority, and even from participating in the electoral process.

The Islamic state's designation of an inferior status to non-Muslim citizens, and discrimination against them on ideological grounds is judged to be humane and equitable. Mawdudi defended the Islamic system for being the most just, the most tolerant and the most generous of all systems in its treatment of national minorities that disagree with the prevailing ideology.[104]

Islamic Policies

As an indispensable agency for the realization of Islamic universalism and totality, the Islamic state is empowered with an authority that is all-embracing and universal in scope. This authority invests the state with the right to command (*amr*) and to prohibit (*nahy*) the followers in all aspects of life. Therefore, the state's ". . . sphere of activity is co-extensive with the whole of human life. It seeks to mould every aspect of life and activity in consonance with its moral norms and programme of social reform. In such a state no one can regard any field of his affairs as personal and private."[105] In Mawdudi's view, it is the state's divinely-ordained right and responsibility to exert control over literally everything, as long as the state's actions are based on proper moral and religious principles.

The Islamic state has been criticized for its extensive authorities, because these authorities have proven to be conducive to totalitarianism. For the Islamic state to be democratic, it should allow communal input into decision-making, which would consequently limit the state's authority. However, many students of Islam view the totality and universalism of the state consistent with Islamic democracy, a democracy that is defined in terms of God's will rather than popular sovereignty. Mawdudi asserted that although there seems to be a resemblance between the functions of the Islamic state and totalitarian forms of government, it is inappropriate to reject both good and bad forms of totalitarianism.[106] He argued that the Islamic state is totalitarian because to reflect the universality of the Islamic vision, its authority cannot be limited. However, unlike fascist and communist forms of totalitarianism, Islamic totalitarianism is good because it rejects dictatorship and guarantees individual liberties. According to Mawdudi, as far as the scope of authority is concerned, the Islamic state is a moderate state that enjoys the advantages and avoids the excesses and shortfalls of democracy and totalitarianism. Due to these very features, he labels the Islamic state as a "totalitarian theo-democracy."[107]

The Islamic law clearly aims to establish a balance between the authority of the state and communal rights by accounting for mandatory, prohibited and discretionary or permitted acts. In Mawdudi's view, the Islamic law not only accounts for moderation on the part of the state by considering the largest category of acts as discretionary or permitted, but also sets further limitations on the powers of the state. Therefore, the state should guarantee freedoms of opinion and religion, as long as such rights do not interfere with the state's affairs and do not enhance the imposition of one's ideology on others by force. The state may not deprive anyone of life, honor, property, and personal liberties without specific legal injunctions, just cause and due process.[108]

The socio-economic policies of the Islamic state should develop a well-balanced system of social justice. Achieving this justice, Mawdudi observed, requires the eradication of all forms of evil and the advancement of all types of virtue and excellence expressed in the Quran. In this pursuit, Mawdudi suggested, ". . . political power will be made use of as and when the occasion demands; all means of propaganda and peaceful persuasion will be employed; the moral education of the people will also be undertaken; and social influence as well as the force of public opinion will be harnessed to the task."[109]

Pursuit and supremacy of justice, respect for commitment, reciprocity, universal brotherhood, peaceful coexistence and universal Islamization are the main principles governing Islamic foreign policies, according to the Quran, Muhammad's tradition and a host of scholarly writings. The Quran commands all Muslims to be just under all circumstances.[110] In the pursuit of a universal justice, Qutb maintained that ". . . Muslims must combat oppression and injustice wherever they are found . . ."[111] Islam explicitly recognizes violence as an acceptable tool for the preservation of justice and the destruction of the unjust. The Islamic holy war (*jihad*) is a means of destroying existing unjust sovereign political systems.

However, the Islamic state is required to honor its contractual commitments even with the unjust regimes. The Quran specifically commands Muslims to honor their pacts, even with their potential enemies, for the sake of peace. Muslims should not dissolve their treaties with pagans, unless they have broken them unilaterally.[112] Muhammad is believed to have said "Three are equally binding upon you whether the other party is a believer or non-believer: contracts, Trusts, and family obligations."[113]

Reciprocity is required not only in contractual commitments but also in the overall conduct of relations with others, since it contributes ". . . to the promotion and establishment of a sane, progressive and viable world-order."[114] This commits the Islamic state to the principle of human brotherhood and peaceful coexistence. According to the Quran, God commands Muslims to deal with others justly and kindly, ". . . for God loves those who are just."[115]

Islam asks the entire humanity to live in peace. War and violence is only permitted to deter injustice and aggression.[116] According to Khomeini, it is the duty of all Islamic states and nations to revolt against super power aggression, and to preserve the independence of their states and the freedom of their nations.[117] This cannot be achieved without the unity and strength of the Islamic state. Violence is not permitted as a means of promoting Islam. The Islamic state should preach and promote Islam by peaceful means, and resort to violence only if it is denied these rights.

NOTES

1. Muhammad Iqbal, "Islam as a Moral and Political Ideal," in *Thoughts and Reflections of Iqbal*, ed. Syed Abdul Vahid (Lahore: Ashraf Press, 1964), 35-38, 50.

2. Ali Shariati, *Islam Shinasi* (Mashhad: N.p., 1347 A.H.), 75-76.

3. John L. Esposito, "Introduction: Islam and Muslim Politics," in *Voices of Resurgent Islam*, ed. John L. Esposito (New York: Oxford University Press, 1983), 4, 5.

4. Godfrey H. Jansen, *Militant Islam* (New York: Harper and Row, 1979), 17.

5. Bernard Lewis, "The Return of Islam," in *Religion and Politics in the Middle East*, ed. Michael Curtis (Boulder: Westview Press, 1981), 12.

6. Jansen, *Militant Islam*, 12. (Press Conference in Cairo, April 1972.)

7. Erwin I. J. Rosenthal, "Some Reflections on the Separation of Religion and Politics in Modern Islam," *Islamic Studies* 3 (September 1964): 278, 277, 275.

8. Ruhullah Khomeini, *Balagh, Farmayeshat-i Mowsui-i Hazrat-i Imam Khomeini, Rahbar-i Kabir-i Inqilab va Boniangozar-i Jomhoori-i Islami*, 1358 A.H., vol. 1 (Tehran: Tehran Publishing House, 1361 A.H.), 105, 110.

9. Ruhullah Khomeini, *Payamha va Sokhanraniha-ye Imam Khomeini, dar sheshmahe-ye dowom-i sal-i 1359*, vol. 2 (Tehran: Noor Publications, n.d.), 98.

10. Ruhullah Khomeini, *Payamha va Sokhanraniha-ye Imam Khomeini az Shahrivar-i 1320 ta Hejrat be Paris*, vol. 5 (Tehran: Noor Publications, 1361 A.H.), 204-205.

11. Ruhullah Khomeini, *Balagh, Sokhanan-i Mowsui-i Imam Khomeini* (Tehran: Sepehr Publishing House, 1362 A.H.), 27.

12. Ibid., 29.

13. Ibid., 28.

14. Khomeini, *Payamha va Sokhanraniha-ye Imam Khomeini*, 5:210.

15. Khomeini, *Payamha va Sokhanraniha-ye Imam Khomeini*, 2:192-193.

16. Ali Shariati, *Ummat va Imamate, Ja-al-Haq, The Collection of Speeches* (Tehran: Husayniyyah-i Irshad, 1351 A.H.), 64.

17. Abul A'la Mawdudi, *Islamic Law and Constitution*, trans. Khurshid Ahmad (Lahore: Islamic Publications, 1967), 165.

18. Cited in Charles J. Adams, "Mawdudi and the Islamic State," in *Voices of Resurgent Islam*, ed. John L. Esposito (New York: Oxford University Press, 1983), 113-114.

19. Quoted in Yvonne Y. Haddad, "Sayyid Qutb: Ideologue of Islamic Revival," in *Voices of Resurgent Islam*, ed. John L. Esposito (New York: Oxford University Press, 1983), 86.

20. Sayyid Qutb, *Hadha al-Din* (Cairo: Dar al-Qalam, 1962), 34.

21. Qutb, *Maalim fi al-Tariq* (Cairo: Maktabat Wahbah, 1964), 64.

22. Ali 'Abd al-Raziq, "The Caliphate and the Basis of Power," in *Islam in Transition, Muslim Perspectives*, ed. John J. Donohue and John L. Esposito (New York: Oxford University Press, 1982), 30-37.

23. Manzooruddin Ahmed, "Key Political Concepts in the Quran," *Islamic Studies* 10 (June 1971): 85.

24. Mawdudi, *Islamic Law and Constitution*, 175, 177.

25. Ruhullah Khomeini, *Hukumat-i Islami* (Najaf: Nahzat-i Islami Series, 1971), 29.

26. Ali Shariati, *Tashayyo-i Alavi va Tashayyo-i Safavi* (Tehran: Student Library of the College of Literature and Humanities, 1352 A.H.), 37-39.

27. Michael M. J. Fischer, "Imam Khomeini: Four Levels of Understanding," in *Voices of Resurgent Islam*, ed. John L. Esposito (New York: Oxford University Press, 1983), 171.

28. Shariati, *Tashayyo-i Alavi va Tashayyo-i Safavi*, 46.

29. Muhammad Asad, *The Principles of State and Government in Islam* (Berkeley: University of California Press, 1961), 1.

30. Ibid., 21.

31. Asad, *The Principles of State*, 23.

32. Hamid Behzadi, "The Principles of Legitimacy and Its Influence Upon the Muslim Political Theory," *Islamic Studies* 10 (December 1971): 280.

33. Fauzi M. Najjar, "Democracy in Islamic Political Philosophy," *Studia Islamica* 51 (1980): 116.

34. Khomeini, *Balagh, Sokhanan-i Mowsui-i Imam Khomeini*, 37.

35. Khomeini, *Balagh, Farmayeshat-i Mowsui-i Hazrat-i Imam Khomeini*, 1:1, 5.
36. Quoted in Fazlur Rahman, "Some Aspects of Iqbal's Political Thought," *Studies in Islam* 5 (July 1968): 165.
37. Shariati, *Ummat va Imamate*, 162, 182.
38. Shariati, *Tashayyo-i Alavi va Tashayyo-i Safavi*, 273-274.
39. Fazlur Rahman, "The Islamic Concept of State," in *Islam in Transition, Muslim Perspectives*, ed. John J. Donohue and John L. Esposito (New York: Oxford University Press, 1982), 263.
40. Abul A'la Mawdudi, "Political Theory of Islam," in *Islam in Transition, Muslim Perspectives*, ed. John Donohue and John L. Esposito (New York: Oxford University Press, 1982), 254.
41. Rahman, "The Islamic Concept of State," 270.
42. Quoted in Haddad, "Sayyid Qutb," 72.
43. Quoted in Haddad, "Sayyid Qutb," 72.
44. Haddad, "Sayyid Qutb," 70.
45. Quoted in Haddad, "Sayyid Qutb," 70.
46. Haddad, "Sayyid Qutb," 71.
47. Sayyid Qutb, *Nahwa Mujtama Islami*, 2nd ed. (Beirut: Dar al-Shuruq, 1975), 47, 50 and 64.
48. Quoted in Haddad, "Sayyid Qutb," 76.
49. Quoted in Haddad, "Sayyid Qutb," 74.
50. Sayyid Qutb, *Khasais al-Tasawwur al-Islami wa-muqawwamatuhu* (Cairo: Issa al-Babi al-Halabi wa-Shurakauhu, 1962), 83.
51. Haddad, "Sayyid Qutb," 75.
52. Quoted in Haddad, "Sayyid Qutb," 76.
53. Quran, 12:40.
54. Quran, 3:154.
55. Quran, 4:64.
56. Quran, 6:50.
57. Mawdudi, *Islamic Law and Constitution*, 217-219.
58. Ibid., 53.
59. Mawdudi, "Political Theory of Islam," 254.
60. Khomeini, *Balagh, Farmayeshat-i Mowsui-i Hazrat-i Imam Khomeini*, 1:23-24, 73.
61. Ibid., 76.
62. Khomeini, *Balagh, Sokhanan-i Mowsui-i Imam Khomeini*, 138.
63. *Kamnimeh Khabarnameh*, No. 17 (Najaf: National Front of Iran Publications, June 1978), 13.
64. Ruhullah Khomeini, *Nameh-i az Imam-i Mussavi, Kashif al-Ghita* (Tehran: N.p., 1356 A.H.), 52-53.
65. Javid Iqbal, "Democracy and the Modern Islamic State," in *Voices of Resurgent Islam*, ed. John L. Esposito (New York: Oxford University Press, 1983), 257.
66. Asad, *The Principles of State*, 51-52.
67. Khomeini, *Kashif al-Ghita*, 53-54.

68. Ruhullah Khomeini, "Islamic Government," in *Islam in Transition, Muslim Perspectives*, ed. John J. Donohue and John L. Esposito (New York: Oxford University Press, 1982), 317.
69. For specific Quranic injunctions and the *Hadith* regarding recruitment to positions of authority see Mawdudi, *Islamic Law and Constitution*, 255, 281-282.
70. Adams, "Mawdudi and the Islamic State," 124.
71. Mawdudi, *Islamic Law and Constitution*, 77.
72. Ibid., 78.
73. Adams, "Mawdudi and the Islamic State," 126-127.
74. Khomeini, *Hukumat-i Islami*, 62.
75. A. K. Brohi, *Islam in the Modern World*, 2nd ed., ed. Khurshid Ahmad (Lahore: Publisher United Ltd., 1975), 101.
76. Ayatullah Mahmud Taliqani, "The Characteristics of Islamic Economics," in *Islam in Transition, Muslim Perspectives*, ed. John J. Donohue and John L. Esposito (New York: Oxford University Press, 1982), 215.
77. Quran, 7:29.
78. Khomeini, *Balagh, Farmayeshat-i Mowsui-i Hazrat-i Imam Khomeini*, 1:33, 1:78, and 1:193.
79. Brohi, *Islam in the Modern World*, 104.
80. Quran, 6:165 and 43:32.
81. Abul Hasan Bani-Sadr, "Islamic Economics: Ownership and Tawhid," in *Islam in Transition, Muslim Perspectives*, ed. John J. Donohue and John L. Esposito (New York: Oxford University Press, 1982), 230, 234.
82. Taliqani, "The Characteristics of Islamic Economics," 210.
83. Bani-Sadr, "Islamic Economics: Ownership and Tawhid," 231.
84. Taliqani, "The Characteristics of Islamic Economics," 212.
85. Quran, 62:10.
86. Quoted in Haddad, "Sayyid Qutb," 93.
87. Quran, 73:20, 4:32, 104:2, 28:77, 81, 83.
88. Quoted in M. 'Umar Chapra, "The Islamic Welfare State," in *Islam in Transition, Muslim Perspectives*, ed. John J. Donohue and John L. Esposito (New York: Oxford University Press, 1982), 224.
89. Brohi, *Islam in the Modern World*, 105.
90. Mustafa Mahmud, "Islam vs. Marxism and Capitalism," in *Islam in Transition, Muslim Perspectives*, ed. John J. Donohue and John L. Esposito (New York: Oxford University Press, 1982), 158.
91. Brohi, *Islam in the Modern World*, 109.
92. Ibid., 115.
93. A. K. Brohi, "The Concept of Islamic Socialism," in *Islam in Transition, Muslim Perspectives*, ed. John J. Donohue and John L. Esposito (New York: Oxford University Press, 1982), 138.
94. Khurshid Ahmad, "Islam and the Challenge of Economic Development," in *Islam in Transition, Muslim Perspectives*, ed. John J. Donohue and John L. Esposito (New York: Oxford University Press, 1982), 218-219.
95. Haddad, "Sayyid Qutb," 92.
96. Mawdudi, *Islamic Law and Constitution*, 50.

97. Khomeini, *Balagh Farmayeshat-i Mowsui-i Hazrat-i Imam Khomeini*, 1:32.
98. Ibid., 1:111.
99. Shaykh Muhammad Husayn Na'ini, "Islam and Constitutional Government," in *Islam in Transition, Muslim Perspectives*, ed. John J. Donohue and John L. Esposito (New York: Oxford University Press, 1982), 291.
100. Khalid M. Ishaque, "The Islamic Approach to Economic Development," in *Voices of Resurgent Islam*, ed. John L. Esposito (New York: Oxford University Press, 1983), 274.
101. Adams, "Mawdudi and the Islamic State," 122.
102. Mawdudi, *Islamic Law and Constitution*, 155.
103. Adams, "Mawdudi and the Islamic State," 121.
104. Ibid., 122.
105. Mawdudi, *Islamic Law and Constitution*, 154.
106. Ibid., 154-155.
107. Adams, "Mawdudi and the Islamic State," 120.
108. Mawdudi, *Islamic Law and Constitution*, 266-268.
109. Mawdudi, "Political Theory of Islam," 256.
110. Quran, 5:8.
111. Quoted in Haddad, "Sayyid Qutb," 84.
112. Quran, 5:13, 9:4, 7.
113. Quoted in al-Sadiq al-Mahdi, "Islam—Society and Change," in *Voices of Resurgent Islam*, ed. John L. Esposito (New York: Oxford University Press, 1983), 238.
114. Rahman, "The Islamic Concept of State," 271.
115. Quran, 60:8.
116. Quran, 2:208, 22:39.
117. Khomeini, *Balagh, Farmayeshat-i Mowsui-i Hazrat-i Imam Khomeini*, 1:17 and 1:29.

3

The Politics of Islamic Sectarianism

Shortly after Muhammad's death, the Islamic community was divided over the question of succession to the prophet. This division, which was initially political in nature, gradually developed into sectarian disputes involving theological and socio-political issues. Consequently, Islamic sectarianism explains both political developments in the Islamic community and major changes in the theological interpretations of Islamic principles.

This and the ensuing chapters focus on the political dimension of sectarian trends in the Islamic community. It will be argued that communal disputes over such political questions as qualifications of leaders, their modes of succession to power and their relationship with their followers were the main sources of sectarianism. Initially, sectarianism did not seem disuniting. In fact, it provided the necessary flexibility for expansion of the Islamic ideology to various lands and its fusion with other belief systems. However, later developments within the two major sects of Sunnism and Shi'ism gradually transformed Islamic sectarianism into a disintegrating force in the Islamic community.

MONOLITHICISM AND SECTARIANISM

Islam sanctions the unity of the community of believers. Theoretically speaking, such a unity is the logical consequence of the totality, universality and centrality of Islam deriving from the totality of God and His message. Islamic monolithicism is theoretically the consequence of the doctrine of oneness (*tawhid*). Unity is also a practical necessity for the preservation of Islam and the protection of its believers in the face of external challenge and aggression. Disunity is not only incompatible with the basic premises of Islam, but also endangers the survival and growth of the Islamic community.

Despite frequent calls for unity, disunity in the Islamic community grew out of sectarian and ethno-national tendencies after Muhammad's demise. Initial divisions, which were mainly political in nature, seemed not only acceptable, but even necessary and logical consequences of the rapid spread of Islam to culturally heterogeneous peoples. As a matter of fact, the survival and growth of Islam required flexibility in integrating different groups and incorporating their ideas into the unified mainstream of Islamic thinking. The initial division between Sunnism and Shi'ism did ". . . not contradict its [the Islamic religious tradition's] inner unity and transcendence. Rather it has been the way of ensuring spiritual unity in a world of diverse cultural and ethnic backgrounds."[1] In their original make-up, Sunnism and Shi'ism, though different, were both accurate interpretations of Islam since they belonged to Islam's total orthodoxy and ensured its unity and totality. The division between Sunnism and Shi'ism, according to Seyyed Hossein Nasr, was not disuniting because it did not entail the destruction of Islamic principles and forms, nor its continuity. More than any other worldwide religious tradition, Nasr asserts, Islam displayed homogeneity, and sectarianism facilitated the participation of a larger community with different traditions in Islam.[2] In support of Shi'ism, which has frequently been blamed for causing disunity in the Islamic community, Shi'i scholars have emphatically argued that Shi'ism did not destroy the unity of Islam; instead, it contributed to Islam's historical development and success.

The original dispute between the two sects was of ". . . a *Fekri* [matter of opinion], scientific, and historical nature over the accurate understanding of the reality of Islam . . ."[3] In opposition to the choice of Abu-Bakr as the prophet's successor, those who later came to be known as the Shi'is insisted that recognizing the reality of Islam requires following Muhammad and his rightful descendants. Therefore, they developed distinct doctrines of leadership (*imamah*) and divine justice (*'adl*) and incorporated these doctrines into the basic principles of Islam (*usul ad-din*) that, according to the Sunnis, only include the oneness of God (*tawhid*), prophecy of Muhammad (*nubuwwah*) and return (*ma'ad*).

The dispute over the question of authority developed out of disagreements about two major questions: Did the prophet of Islam intend to appoint a successor for himself or not? And if not, should the choice of leadership be left to the community? According to the Sunnis, who based their argument on the Quranic doctrines of *shura* and *ijma*, Muhammad's intent in his declaration of support for Ali at Ghadir Khum was not to appoint a successor. Quranic injunctions and the Arab historical practices, which left the choice of leadership to the community, made the appointment of Ali unlikely and even improper. As reflected in the doctrines of *shura* and *ijma*, the Quran explicitly commands the believers to consult with each other and develop a consensus in managing their affairs. Since the Quran was not specific about the choice of leadership, the Sunnis relied on Arab tribal practices, and the institution of *al-Nadawa* was used for the choice of Abu-Bakr.

To the Shi'is, the issue of authority was of great importance. For them the question of who should succeed the prophet was closely tied to the function of leadership. The Shi'i imam's function was to rule over the community in justice and be able to interpret the Divine Law and its esoteric meaning. Indeed, unlike the Sunni caliphs who gradually shifted towards temporal power and abandoned their role as spiritual leaders, the Shi'i imams always maintained their role as the interpreters of the Divine Law. Hence, according to the Shi'is, the nature of the imams' functions requires them to be free from error and sin (*ma'sum*) and this means that they should be chosen by divine decree (*nass*) through the prophet.[4] The Quran, *Hadith* and Muhammad's *Sunnah* indicated to the Shi'is that Muhammad not only had the right to appoint his successor, but he had actually done so by appointing Ali to the leadership of the community.

The Quran explicitly recognizes Muhammad's authority by commanding Muslims: ". . . whatsoever the Messenger give you, take it. And whatsoever he forbids, abstain [from it]."[5] The Quran also says, "Verily in the messenger of Allah you have a good example . . ."[6] A host of Muhammad's *hadiths*, according to the Shi'is, indicate his preference for Ali as his successor. Referring to Ali, the prophet is believed to have said: "This is my brother, my trustee and my successor among you, so listen to him and obey."[7] The *Hadith* also cites Muhammad at Ghadir Khum asking the people: "Do you not acknowledge that I have a greater claim on each of the believers than they have on themselves?" After their positive response, Muhammad raised Ali's hand and said: "Of whomever I am Lord [*mawla*] then Ali is also his Lord. O God! Be thou the supporter of whoever supports Ali and the enemy of whoever opposes him." In a Sunni collection of *hadiths*, Ahmad ibn Hanbal claims that after the Ghadir Khum incident, Umar ibn Khattab, the second Rightly-Guided Caliph, met Ali and told him: "Congratulation, O son of Abu Talib! Now morning and evening [i.e. forever] you are the master of every believing man and woman." In the *hadith* of *al-Thaqalayan* (The Two Worthy Matters), Muhammad is also believed to have said:

> I have left among you two worthy matters which if you cling to them you shall not be led into error after me. One of them is greater than the other: The Book of God which is a rope stretched from Heaven to Earth

and my progeny, the people of my house [*ahl al-bayt*]. These two shall not be parted until they return to the pool [of paradise].⁸

Muhammad expressed a similar preference for his family to succeed him in the *hadith* of *Safinah* (Noah's Ark) by saying: "My family among you are like Noah's Ark. He who sails on it will be safe, but he who holds back from it will perish."⁹

The choice of Ali, in the Shi'i view, was mainly due to his special and unique virtues, his services to Islam and Muhammad's fear of adverse consequences of an elective process that might lead to the choice of incompetent and corrupt successors, and consequently to chaos. Ali was praised by Muhammad and others for his brevity, truthfulness, knowledge and his popularity with the followers.

The prophet recognized the need for permanent leadership and never failed to appoint a temporary replacement to rule in his absence whenever he left Medina. He had traditionally relied on Ali's assistance for the management of communal affairs. During the Medinan period Ali was entrusted with sensitive responsibilities and acted as Muhammad's secretary and deputy. It was, therefore, inconsistent with Muhammad's practice not to appoint a successor to direct the affairs of the community after his death. Shi'is believe that even if Muhammad had intended to leave the choice of leadership to the community, ". . . still it would be necessary for the prophet to give an explanation concerning this matter."¹⁰

These initial disputes over the question of succession gradually evolved into fundamentally distinct leadership doctrines. The doctrine of *khalifah*, advocated by the Sunnis, relied on the elective method for the choice of leadership and, with the gradual bureaucratization of the *khalifah* system, accepted the separation of temporal authority from spiritual authority. Recognizing Muhammad's right to choose his successor from his own family, Shi'is developed the doctrines of *imamah* which emphasized the appointive method of leadership succession. According to these doctrines, the Shi'i imams must be knowledgeable (*'alim*) and sinless (*ma'sum*), and should perform the threefold function of ruling over the community as Muhammad's representative, interpreting the esoteric (*batini*) meaning of religious sciences and law and guiding followers in their spiritual lives. These doctrinal gaps sharpened sectarian disputes not only over such leadership questions as leaders' functions, qualifications, succession and relationships with their followers, but also over more fundamental theological and juridical issues including the sources of Divine Law, occultation, etc.

ISLAMIC SECTARIANISM: FOUNDATIONS, DEVELOPMENTS AND IMPLICATIONS

Whether sectarianism in Islam was simply a political phenomenon centered around the question of authority or a more complex religio-political division in the community, its political importance cannot be overestimated. The Islamic message was originally brought to the Arabs and in its initial evolution was influenced by pre-Islamic Arab and non-Arab traditions. In their efforts to spread Islam, Arabs expanded the Islamic community by assimilating into the overwhelmingly Arab Islamic community various ethno-national groups that were ". . . neither homogeneous in cultural backgrounds and tradition nor in politico-social institutions."[11] As a result, a multiplicity of approaches and points of view on non-fundamental and mostly political issues developed in this growing community. The majority of Arab followers, who later came to be known as Sunnis, were primarily influenced by pre-Islamic Arab and non-Arab traditions and institutions as well as Islamic principles in developing their religio-political doctrines. Thus, the Quranic doctrines of *shura* and *ijma;* and the Arab traditional institution of *al-Nadawa*, which was the historical means for the choice of Arab tribal leaders, became the main theoretical and practical sources of the doctrine of *khalifah*.

Shi'ism, which was originally a political movement, gradually evolved into a complex ideological, religious, and socio-political movement by drawing upon diverse sources. It is often inaccurately concluded that Shi'ism is nothing more than a reinterpretation of Islam initiated by Iranians and adapted to their historical and socio-political traditions. According to Ignaz Goldziher, "There is a fallacy that the emergence and development of the Shia represents a modification of Islam by ideas of the Iranian peoples that conquest or missionary activity had brought into the Muslim community."[12] In fact, Shi'ism and its doctrines of *imamah* that emphasized hereditary succession to the rule had their roots in the Arab, Islamic, pre-Islamic Persian, Greco-Alexandrian, gnostic, Chinese and Indian thoughts and traditions. However, Arabs created Shi'ism and gave it its Arabic name, meaning "partisans," referring to the Shi'is' support for Ali's leadership after the prophet. ". . . The extremist apotheosis of Ali was first proclaimed by 'Abdallah ibn Saba—before there could be any question of an influx of such ideas from an Aryan environment . . ."[13] The Arab support for Shi'ism and its doctrine of hereditary succession was partly the result of the Arabs' historical experiences with monarchism. Hereditary succession was not a novelty to the South Arabians who as an ancient civilization had long experienced monarchism. "Even if the seventh-century Arabs had no personal experience of kingship, they came from the land of a civilization based on charismatic leaders, and must somehow have been influenced by a continuing tradition"[14] In the seventh and even later centuries, the appointive (*wisayah*) method of leadership succession based on inheritance was accepted and practiced by the Shi'i and Sunni Arabs mainly because leadership based on inherited qualities was an inalienable element of Arab traditional socio-political practices. In the Arab society of the time, social status depended upon inherited qualities. Arabs believed that individuals inherit their physical and moral qualities from their ancestors. Thus, socio-political mobility in tribal Arab societies was based upon inherited qualities. In the monarchic institution of *Mukarrib* in South Arabia, for example, where political and religious authority were merged into the office of priest-king, leaders were appointed on the basis of their inheritance.[15] Here, non-inherited personal qualities were of little consequence. Similarly, Muhammad's support for a fusion of temporal and religious authority and his insistence upon a legitimist approach to succession in order to keep leadership in his family were congruent with these Arab traditions. After the prophet, Arabs with similar theocratic and legitimist leanings joined the Shi'i movement making it ". . . quite as Arab in its roots as Islam itself."[16]

The expansion of Islam to non-Arab lands and its exposure to other belief systems resulted in a reciprocal interaction between Islamic and non-Islamic ideas that enabled Islam to influence, and be influenced by, the alien Greek, Persian, Indian and Chinese ideas as long as these ideas were inwardly related to Islam.

This reciprocal influence is nowhere more apparent than in the link between Shi'ism and Persian socio-political thought. Although Arabs created Shi'ism and played a pivotal role in its early development, many Persians converted to Shi'ism much before Shi'ism was adopted as the official religion of Iran by the Safavids in 1501. Pro-Shi'i Sufi orders and craft guilds in Iran prepared the populace to accept Shi'ism under the Safavids, and early Iranian scholars including ibn Babuyah and Shaykhu't-Ta'ifa were instrumental in the early development of the Shi'i thought.

Ever since the adoption of Shi'ism as the official religion of Iran, the Persian soul has had an intimate link with Shi'ism, and Persian sociopolitical thought has played at least a secondary role in the development of the Shi'i political doctrines. By integrating their pre-Islamic Zoroastrian and Mazdaki beliefs into the Islamic universal perspectives, Persians assisted in building an Islamic civilization founded upon an Islamic ideology containing Persian values.[17] Persians' stress on their own cultural values was not only conducive to a distinct Persian Islamic culture, but also influenced Shi'i Arabs' religio-political doctrines particularly in reasserting the notion of divine-right monarchism.

As an essential element of the pre-Islamic Persian belief system, Zoroastrianism was introduced to and absorbed by this new Islamic culture of Iran. However, the integration of the dualistic Zoroastrian thought (Good versus Evil) into the monolithic Islamic belief system required a fundamental transformation in Zoroastrianism. The *Ishraqi* (Illuminationist) doctrine that rapidly spread among Persian Shi'is entailed certain elements of Zoroastrianism. However, Shihab ad-Din Suhrawardi, who advanced the *Ishraqi* ideas and relied on the Zoroastrian symbolism of light and darkness, rejected dualism and the exoteric teachings of Zoroastrians. He possessed an esoteric doctrine based on the Unity of the Divine Principle and sided with those Zoroastrians who advocated some form of monolithicism.[18] Zoroastrian influence is also apparent among such Shi'i factions as *Ismailiyyah* and *Ishaqiyyah* (*Khurramiyyah* or *Khurramdiniyyah*). The *Ishraqis* elevated Zoroastrianism to the point of contending that Abu-Muslim, a general of the Abbasid dynasty, was in fact a prophet sent by Zoroaster to revive his religion. Zoroastrian dualism can also be traced in the non-orthodox and literary works by Iranian Shi'is. In the famous Persian literary work, *Shahnameh*, Abul Qasim Ferdowsi, a Muslim, acknowledged dualism by identifying good with God (*Allah*) and bad with the Quranic *Iblis* (devil).

Judeo-Christian and gnostic thoughts and traditions also figured in the development of Shi'ism. For instance, the doctrine of *imamah* with its messianic element and opposition to the secular view of the state's power corresponds to Judeo-Christian thought. The *Ismailis*, whose preoccupation with a form of arithmetical symbolism has made their doctrine of leadership distinct from that of other Shi'is, are influenced by Gnosticism. The Greek philosophical traditions, especially the more esoteric schools connected with neo-Pythagoreanism and Hermeticism, also played a formative role in Shi'ism and Sufism.[19] The Shi'i school of Isfahan, for example, emphasized both rational and intuitive aspects of the mind characteristic of Aristotelian philosophy. Neo-Platonic thought has not only been influential in the *Ismaili* and Sufi schools, but also in Khomeini's recent doctrine of *vilayat-i faqih* (leadership of the jurisprudent). To advance their own brand of Shi'ism, the Twelver ulama, particularly Muhammad Baqir Majlisi and Shaykh Muhammad al-Hurr al-'Amili during the Safavids, downgraded and effectively reduced the role of Greek philosophy and Sufism in Shi'ism. This anti-philosophical dogmatism still dominates the Twelver clerical establishment despite the recent emergence of neo-Platonic ideas among the Twelvers in the form of *vilayat-i faqih*.

This diversity of sources combined with more fundamental sociopolitical considerations in the Shi'i and Sunni communities not only sharpened the Shi'i-Sunni polemics over political and theological issues but also affected forms and rituals. Moreover, these influences contributed to intense factionalization within the two sects. The Sunni-Shi'i division is reflected in the Shi'i rituals of passion play (*ta'ziyah*) and *rawda-kha[w]ni*. These rituals which emphasize Husayn's martyrdom at the hands of the oppressive Sunni majority have not only consolidated the Shi'i identity and facilitated its growth, they have also enabled the Shi'is to project themselves as the oppressed minority, deprived of its essential and legitimate rights in the Islamic community. There is, however, a paradox in the Shi'i attitude towards this intense discrimination and persecution. Many Shi'is, particularly the Twelvers or *Imami* Shi'is, have embraced political quietism and have praised imams for their *taqiyyah* (religious dissimulation) and patient endurance at the hands of the powerful. At the same time, they have made Husayn the greatest Shi'i hero for his rejection of tyranny and revolt against the oppressors. This paradox has provided Shi'is with an extraordinary political versatility, justifying both political quietism and activism whenever necessary.[20]

The Sunni-Shi'i attitudes towards non-Muslims also characterize the division between them. Generally speaking, contrary to the Sunnis' relatively open and tolerant treatment of non-Muslims, Shi'is maintain a rigid, intolerant and exclusive attitude towards other sects and religions. This behavioral difference might be attributed to the Zoroastrian influences on Shi'ism. As Goldziher suggests, "The treatment of non-Shii in Shii law reminds us immediately of the ancient rules in Persian religious texts. These rules are mostly obsolete among modern Zoroastrians. The Shii attitude may be regarded as their Islamic echo."[21] This attitude is, of course, contradictory to the explicit Quranic instruction regarding treatment of non-Muslims. The Quran says:

> This day are [all] good things made lawful for you. The food of those who have received the scripture is lawful for you, and your food is lawful for them. And so are the virtuous women of the believers and the virtuous women of those who received the scripture before you [lawful for you] when you give them their marriage portions and live with them in honor, not in fornication, nor taking them as secret combines . . ."[22]

A complex set of socio-political developments were also instrumental in transforming both Shi'ism and Sunnism, which were originally not too far apart, into distinct sects and gradually widening their gap. The treatment of Persians by Arabs as second class citizens and suppression of Persian aspirations were major socio-political issues that heightened the tension between Arabs and Persians, and gradually transformed these predominantly ethnic differences into effective disintegrating sectarian conflicts. This growing tension was apparent in the changes within the Shaoobi movement. Initially, the Shaoobi movement stood for a unified Islamic community based upon the equality of Arab and non-Arab (*ajam*) believers. However, as tensions grew, the movement attempted to revitalize ethno-national values that Islam had abandoned since its inception by emphasizing non-Arab superiority over Arabs and by rejecting manifestations of Arab dominance including the *khalifah* system. In this effort, Shaoobies and their Persian supporters attempted to insulate Persian nationalism from Arab cultural milieu and ". . . revitalize the link between Islamic Iran and ancient Iran."[23] Despite its strength, however, the Shaoobi movement failed to spread deeply throughout the Persian socio-political environment mainly as a consequence of the movement's identification with the established political order which lacked much popular support.

Persian monarchs and their allies in the clerical establishment played a determining role in shaping the direction of these developments. Historically speaking, Persian monarchism always aligned itself with religion. To one degree or another, Persian kings rejected secularism and paid homage to religion and its symbols and guardians, including the clerical establishment. The Sasanids (224-651 A.D.) believed that religion and empire are twins or brothers[24] who should cooperate in the pursuit of justice in managing the affairs of the society. In view of this link between religion and politics in monarchic Iran, Islam was to become a political tool available to the political establishment to serve two major purposes: to maintain a separate identity for the Persian empire vis-a-vis the Islamic empire by emphasizing their differences and, more importantly, to legitimize Persian monarchism and monarchs' dynastic rules.

To maintain a separate identity for their empire, Shariati claimed the Safavids (1501-1722 A.D.) adopted Shi'ism and assimilated into their brand of Shi'ism popularly appealing elements of Persian nationalism and Christian thought.[25] Moreover, the Safavids pursued greater collaboration with Christian Europe. The great Safavid monarch, Shah Abbas, entered into economic and political relations with Europeans. The Persians' collaboration with Europeans intensified the rivalry between the Persian and Ottoman empires in the early years of the seventeenth century, and facilitated the establishment of a united Persian-Christian front against the Ottoman empire.

As to the goal of dynastic legitimacy, the Safavids found a strong ally in the Shi'i doctrine of *imamah* because of this doctrine's advocacy of the appointive process for succession to power. They, therefore, adopted

Shi'ism as the official religion of Iran and combined their brand of political authority and legitimacy with that of Shi'ism. The Safavids and subsequent Persian dynasties took every opportunity to develop and strengthen their brand of Shi'ism, particularly its doctrine of *imamah*, as an instrument of legitimizing Persian monarchism and protecting it vis-a-vis its enemies. Hence, Shi'ism gave a religious dimension to Persian monarchism and further enhanced its legitimacy.

In their attempt to link Persian monarchism to Shi'ism, Persians went so far as to suggest that a familial tie had been developed between the two during the Sasanids as a result of a marriage between the prophet's family and the Sasanids. Roger M. Savory explains the roots and significance of this suggestion in the following way:

> Most of the early Shi'is were Arabs, but the Iranians soon adopted the movement as an ideal vehicle for the expression of their protests at being treated as second-class citizens in a largely Arab empire. To the political stem of Shi'ism, the Iranians grafted the legend that Husayn, the younger son of 'Ali, married Shahrbanu, the daughter of Yazdigird III, the last monarch of the Sasanid dynasty overthrown by the Arabs. In this way, Shi'ism was lifted out of its purely Islamic context and linked with the Iranian historical, traditional and nationalist sentiments.[26]

Persians professed that the fruit of this marriage, Ali Zayn al-Abidin, "united in his person the double chain of Imamate and Persian royalty,"[27] and as such provided a religio-political basis for the continued legitimacy of the institution of Persian monarchism. This and similar strategies, designed to fuse Shi'ism with the Persian national consciousness, gradually incorporated the Persian conceptions of hereditary succession and the divine right kinship into Shi'ism, and consequently, broadened the gap between the doctrine of *imamah* in Safavid Shi'ism and the Sunni doctrine of *khalifah*.

Factionalism within Shi'ism and the Safavids' adoption of Twelver, *Ithna 'Ashari*, Shi'ism also intensified the Shi'i-Sunni hostilities and the confrontation between the Persian and Ottoman empires. As Twelver Persians made Husayn and his descendants the manifestation of both Shi'ism and Persian monarchism, Husayn's martyrdom (680 A.D.) at the hands of the Sunnis raised this sectarian tension to its peak. Husayn's death not only influenced Shi'i rituals but also made Shi'ism ". . . a politico-religious movement which rapidly developed its distinctive theological doctrines and system of religious law."[28] This distinct Shi'ism increasingly reflected the Persian culture. As Vladimir Minorsky points out: "Even up to our day, Shiism, with its overtones and its aroma of opposition, of martyrdom, and of revolt, is matched quite well with the

Persian character—a character formed in the course of a long history which is very different from the history of other people nearby."[29] This Safavid brand of Shi'ism, in Shariati's opinion, clearly differed from the original Alid Shi'ism, particularly in regard to the essential elements of the doctrine of *imamah*.[30] With the emergence of an independent clerical establishment and the dominant clerics' dogmatic and formal-legalistic approach to Shi'ism, Safavid Shi'ism gradually minimized the esoteric elements of religion and preoccupied itself with exoteric (*zahiri*) aspects like pilgrimage, prayers, etc.

With the bureaucratization of the Sunni institutions and the Sunnis' growing emphasis on Arabism and Arab superiority, particularly during the Umayyad and Abbasid dynasties, the *khalifah* system was also gradually transformed into an Arab government emphasizing Arabs' distinction from, and superiority over, Persians. Hence, this Umayyad brand of Sunnism, contrary to the original Sunni ideas, further amplified ethno-national and sectarian rivalries in the Islamic community. These developments not only broadened the gap between Sunnism and Shi'ism but also intensified factional disputes.

Sunnism and Shi'ism have often inaccurately been portrayed as monolithic Islamic sects. There is no doubt that disputes over theological and political issues led to internal conflict and fragmentation at the early stages of the evolution of both sects and have, more or less, continued to date. In Sunnism, these disputes have been primarily over juridical issues. Shi'i factions began with Ali's death, drastically increased after the third imam—Husayn—and the majority of them gradually died out within a century. This fragmentation resulted from disputes over such doctrinal issues as the leaders' qualities, succession to rule and functions. Some of the early, and presently extinct, Shi'i sects elevated Muhammad, Ali and their progeny to a divine status. For instance, after Ali, the *Saba'iyyah*, who were doctrinal extremists, not only equated Ali to *Allah* but also believed that he was occulted and would return. Some sects even attached divinity to and accepted the leadership of non-Alids including some Sunni caliphs. For example, *Rawandiyyah* professed the divinity of the Abbasids, and *Muslimiyyah* believed that Abu-Muslim—the Abbasid general—was divine, and claimed that he was concealed and would someday return.[31]

Although some early factions like *Sulaymaniyyah* or *Jaririyyah* accepted the doctrine of consultation and recognized the rights of the community to choose its leaders, an overwhelming majority of Shi'i factions have generally accepted the appointive process. They have, however, differed in terms of the number of imams they recognize and their preferences for different familial lines of Ali for the *imamah* of the community. Generally speaking, after every imam there was a group, usually called *waqifiyyah*, who believed that *imamah* had ceased with that imam, and that imam was concealed and would return in the future to bring justice. The *Zaydis*, who did not recognize any rigid hereditary succession principle, contended that *imamah* belongs to any descendants of Ali and Fatimah—Ali's wife and Muhammad's daughter—who is pious, learned and willing to rise and claim the *imamah*. They, therefore, followed Zayd al-Shahid, the son of Imam as-Sajjad, as the fifth imam. The *Ismailis* (Seveners), who greatly emphasized esoteric aspects of religion, followed a different line of *imamah* by accepting Ismail, the son of imam Ja'far as-Sadiq, as their seventh imam. *Ithna 'Ashari* (Twelver) Shi'is, presently the largest faction, developed out of a broader movement of *Imami* Shi'ism in the ninth century. Twelvers believe in twelve imams, the last of whom—Mahdi—was occulted and is believed to return and bring justice. According to W. Montgomery Watt, temporal rulers favored the Twelvers' messianism because it ended imams' succession with the twelfth imam, by transporting him into a supernatural realm, and removed their claim to temporal authority.[32] This messianic element of the twelver doctrine, though not limited to this faction or to Islam, theoretically justified separation of religion from politics and political quietism. *Ismailiyyah* and *Zaydiyyah*, which initially were active in politics, also gradually adopted quietism.[33] These various sectarian and factional divisions transformed the Islam of unity into an Islam of disunity and conflict.

NOTES

1. Allamah Sayyid Muhammad Husayn Tabataba'i, *Shi'ite Islam*, trans. and ed. Seyyed Hossein Nasr (Albany: State University of New York Press, 1975), 7.

2. Seyyed Hossein Nasr, *Ideals and Realities of Islam* (New York: Frederick A. Praeger Publishers, 1967), 148.

3. Ali Shariati, *Tashayyo-i Alavi va Tashayyo-i Safavi* (Tehran: Student Library of the College of Literature and Humanities, 1352 A.H.), 59.

4. See Tabataba'i, *Shi'ite Islam*, 10.

5. Quran, 59:7.

6. Quran, 33:21.

7. Quoted in Abu Ja'far Muhammad al-Tabari, *Ta'rikh al-Rusul Wa'l-Muluk*, vol. 1, ed. M. J. de Goeje (Leiden: E. J. Brill, 1901), 1172-1173.

8. Quoted in Ahmad ibn Muhammad ibn Hanbal, *Al-Musnad*, vol. 4 (Cairo: Matba'a al-Maymaniyya, 1313 A.H.), 281.

9. Quoted in Ahmad ibn Hajar al-Makki, *Al-Sawa'iq al-Muhriqa*, ed. Abdul-Wahhab 'Abdul Latif (Cairo: Maktabat al-Qahira, 1375 A.H.), 150.

10. Tabataba'i, *Shi'ite Islam*, 176.

11. S. Husain M. Jafri, *Origins and Early Development of Shi'a Islam* (London: Longman Group Ltd., 1979), 3.

12. Ignaz Goldziher, *Introduction to Islamic Theology and Law*, trans. Andras Hamori and Ruth Hamori (Princeton: Princeton University Press, 1981), 211.

13. Ibid., 212.

14. W. Montgomery Watt, "Shi'ism Under the Umayyads," *Journal of the Royal Asiatic Society of Great Britain and Ireland* Parts 3 and 4 (1960): 161.

15. Jafri, *Origins and Early Development of Shi'a Islam*, 7-9.

16. Goldziher, *Introduction to Islamic Theology and Law*, 212.

17. For a detailed discussion see Seyyed Hossein Nasr, *Islam and the Plight of Modern Man* (London: Longman Group Ltd., 1975), 101-121.

18. See Seyyed Hossein Nasr, *Three Muslim Sages: Avicenna—Suhrawardi—Ibn 'Arabi* (Cambridge, Mass.: Harvard University Press, 1964), 60.

19. Seyyed Hossein Nasr, *Science and Civilization in Islam* (Cambridge, Mass.: Harvard University Press, 1968), 72.

20. Moojan Momen, *An Introduction to Shi'i Islam: The History and Doctrines of Twelver Shi'ism* (New Haven: Yale University Press, 1985), 236.

21. Goldziher, *Introduction to Islamic Theology and Law*, 215.

22. Quran, 5:5.

23. Shariati, *Tashayyo-i Alavi va Tashayyo-i Safavi*, 111.

24. F. R. C. Bagley, "Religion and the State in Iran," *Islamic Studies* 10 (March 1971): 1.

25. Shariati, *Tashayyo-i Alavi va Tashayyo-i Safavi*, 205-211.

26. Roger M. Savory, "The Problem of Sovereignty in an Ithna 'Ashari Shi'i State," in *Religion and Politics in the Middle East*, ed. Michael Curtis (Boulder: Westview Press, 1981), 132.

27. Vladimir Minorsky, "The Rupture between Sunni and Shi'a in Islam," *Religion* No. 11 (January 1935): 19.

28. Savory, "The Problem of Sovereignty in an Ithna 'Ashari Shi'i State," 132.

29. Vladimir Minorsky, "Iran: Opposition, Martyrdom, and Revolt," in *Unity and Variety in Muslim Civilization*, ed. Gustave E. Von Grunebaum (Chicago: University of Chicago Press, 1955), 201.

30. Shariati, *Tashayyo-i Alavi va Tashayyo-i Safavi*, 250.

31. Momen, *An Introduction to Shi'i Islam*, 46-48.

32. For a detailed discussion see W. Montgomery Watt, *The Formative Period of Islamic Thought* (Edinburgh: Edinburgh University Press, 1973), 151-175.

33. For a detailed discussion of factionalism in Shi'ism see Momen, *An Introduction to Shi'i Islam*, 11-ff.

4

Islamic Political Leadership: Fundamentalism, Sectarianism and Pragmatism

In the first chapter I proposed that the study of Islamic political leadership should be carried out by a contextual approach which facilitates the study of this leadership as an integral component of the Islamic polity. Very few disputes exist over the ideological foundations, functional features and policy positions of the Islamic state. Major disputes have existed, however, over the question of leadership. Historically speaking, these disputes led to disintegrating sectarian trends, making the issue of political authority the core of sectarian and factional schisms in Islam.

In this chapter, the Islamic theories and practices of political leadership are studied. Despite the general acceptance of the indispensability of leadership, Islamic theories of leadership differ in terms of leaders' qualifications, functions, sources of legitimacy and modes of succession to power. To a large degree, disagreements over these issues reflect the sectarian divisions in the *ummah*. The practice of leadership, however, has not been congruent with leadership theories. As charismatic patriarchal leaders in Islam were replaced by patrimonial ones who increasingly relied on weak bureaucratic apparatuses, the practice of leadership by the Sunnis increasingly reflected some Shi'i doctrinal positions. Bureaucratic patrimonialism superseded charismatic leadership through the overall bureaucratization of political authority. This development widened the gap between the theory and practice of Islamic political leadership. Therefore, as Manzooruddin Ahmed points out, to understand political authority in Islam, ". . . it would be necessary to sort out facts from fiction, theory from practice, and the ideal from the reality."[1]

THE INDISPENSABILITY OF LEADERSHIP

Regardless of their sectarian and even factional schisms, all Muslims recognize the need for leadership of the *ummah*. Different Islamic sects, however, have offered divergent explanations why leadership is necessary. Basically, Sunnism justifies leadership on legal grounds and Shi'ism searches for justification in intellect (*'aql*). Although this divergence of views has had important ramifications for the entire political theory of Islam, Muslims remain steadfast in their belief that the implementation of laws, preservation of order and justice and dynamic management of communal affairs is possible only through leadership.

From this functionalist point of view, then, the necessity of leadership is primarily an outgrowth of the *ummah* and its dynamism. Once the *ummah* is established, the emergence of an organized authority is the first step in its development. As evidenced by Muhammad's and his successors' enormous contributions to the development of the Islamic community, this authority, in turn, plays a pivotal role in the further developments of the *ummah*. These developments rely on the leadership's ability to meet communal needs. Preserving law and order, as the primary communal need, according to Muhammad al-Ghazali, makes the tyranny of an usurping leader preferable to chaos.[2] Khomeini, who found explicit justifications for communal leadership in the Quran and Muhammad's *Sunnah*, also believed that it is reasonable to assume that the *ummah* needs leadership. According to him, "a collection of legal codes is not sufficient for the improvement of the society. For the law to become the source of improvement and success of humanity, there is a need for an executive power."[3] Since leadership is an indispensable component of political authority, Khomeini asserted, God Himself appointed Muhammad and his successors as the executive authority in addition to bestowing the *Shari'ah* upon the community. As Muhammad's rule was necessary, so is the rule of the caliph, Khomeini concluded.[4] Ali Shariati advanced a similar argument by asserting that the concept of *imamah*, which means the leadership of the community towards its collective goals, is implicit in the idea of *ummah*. He argued that the community's survival and proper functioning essentially depend upon a responsible leadership that is committed to the ideals and visions of Islam and to a dynamic and effective pursuit of communal goals.[5]

The *Ithna 'Ashari* Shi'is advocate continuity in leadership, thereby attesting explicitly to the indispensability of leadership to the development of the community. In their view, historically, leadership began with creation and will reach its final stage with the return of the twelfth imam by going through four periods, each complementing the previous one and ensuring the continuity of leadership. During the first period, the period of prophecy (*nubuwwah*) which started with Adam and continued through Muhammad's prophecy, leadership belonged to the messengers of God. This period was followed by the period of *imamah*, a period that began with Ali and ended with the minor occultation of Mahdi, during which leadership belonged to the twelve imams and Mahdi's deputies. The Shi'is have not developed a general theory of leadership for the third period that began with the major occultation of Mahdi and continues until the day of resurrection. Some suggest that leadership is the responsibility of the public, others prefer the leadership of a few enlightened and learned individuals. A universal revolution will commence the final period of leadership by facilitating Mahdi's return. At this stage, Mahdi is charged with the leadership which will implement justice in the society.[6]

Abul A'la Mawdudi's great-man theory—a mechanistic theory of leadership—also attributes the indispensability of leadership to the need for societal change and dynamism. He asserts that since the character of any social order flows from the top down, leadership necessarily determines the direction of the society. Thus, the quality of leadership lies exclusively in the leader and his moral orientations rather than socio-economic, political and institutional considerations. Inequality, injustice and suffering in the society then reflect the leader's lack of moral fortitude or his inability, or unwillingness, to deal with these problems. The following passage illustrates Mawdudi's belief in the absolute necessity of a moral and committed leadership at all times:

> What we need is a group of people—a leadership—which is imbued with the spirit of Islam and which is determined to establish Islam, come what may. We all know that if a building has to be constructed, the objective cannot be achieved if the architects who *know* the design of the building and have the *will* to construct it and possess the *requisite resources* are not available. On the other hand if they are available anything can be built—be it a temple or a mosque.[7]

SECTARIANISM AND POLITICAL LEADERSHIP

The issue of leadership has been a primary source of dissonance within the *ummah*. As discussed in the previous chapter, a major dispute developed over the question of succession to the prophet at the time of his demise. While this political controversy gradually led to fundamental theological disputes, particularly as Islam spread to new lands and subsequently non-Islamic beliefs were incorporated into the Islamic vision, the issue of leadership remained the crux of sectarian and factional disputes in Islam. The two major sects, Sunnism and Shi'ism, gradually developed their distinct leadership doctrines which vary significantly in their explanations of the origins, scope and nature of leadership. Gradually, each sect also fell victim to further disputes over these issues and became increasingly fragmented.

The Sunni Doctrine of *Khalifah*

In Sunnism, *khalifah* refers primarily to the institution that is charged with the leadership of the *ummah* after the prophet. This leadership doctrine stems from two Sunni doctrines:

1. Doctrine of delegation, which considers leadership as a delegated right from God—the absolute Sovereign—and man—His vicegerents—to the leader; and
2. Doctrine of obligation, which makes it incumbent upon the followers to obey their leaders, since leaders' authority derives from God's absolute sovereignty.

In the text of the Quran, *Hadith* and other legal and historical documents of Islam frequent references have been made to *khalifah*, *imamah* and their numerous equivalents and derivatives. The synonymous and interchangeable uses of *khalifah* and *imamah* in these texts have not only caused conceptual ambiguity but have also confounded the distinct doctrines of *khalifah* and *imamah*. Etymologically, the concept of *khalifah* derives its source from the term *khalafa*, meaning "coming after someone." In the political terminology of Sunnism, *khalifah* refers to the prophet's and his successors' temporal rule rather than their religious leadership.[8] The caliph is the person who fulfills this role. The imam or the "one who is in front," however, is basically a person who leads congregational prayers, although leaders have also been referred to as imams in Sunnism. In Sa'd ad-Din Taftazani's treatise, *Shahr al-Maqasid*, the imam's role is described as the "general authority that the successor of the prophet holds in the sphere of religious and temporal affairs." Also, in ibn Human's *Musayyarah*, *khalifah* and *imamah* are used interchangeably in reference to "the possession of the full and complete authority over the Islamic community."[9]

The caliph's authority is delegated to him from God, who is the ultimate and absolute sovereign, through his vicegerents. Therefore, the doctrine of delegation, as the essential component of the Sunni doctrine of *khalifah*, rules out man's absolute sovereignty. Absolute sovereignty belongs to God, and God alone is the source of authority in the Islamic community. According to Mawdudi, the prerogative of command belongs to God, and no one is obliged to carry orders that are issued by man in his own right since man is not entitled to such a prerogative.[10] Similarly, Sayyid Qutb attributed absolute sovereignty to God by asserting that:

> There is no ruler save God, no legislator, no organizer of human life and of human relationships to the world, to living things or human beings save God. From Him alone is received all guidance and legislation, all systems of life, norms governing relationships and the measure of values.[11]

The doctrine of delegation is antithetical to the doctrine of popular sovereignty. Muslims' daily confessions that "there is no God but God" is indeed an admission of God's absolute sovereignty and a rejection of any form of human sovereignty. As Mawdudi asserted, the cap of sovereignty was never intended for man, and therefore, it never fits him.[12] However, as vicegerent of God, man is charged with implementing God's will on earth. According to the Quran, the entire Muslim community and its leadership is appointed as God's vicegerents.[13] Muhammad's *Hadith* also affirms human vicegerency. The prophet is believed to have said: "Everyone of you is a ruler and everyone is answerable for his subjects."[14]

Prophecy, according to this doctrine, is a means of presenting God's message to man, and affirming man's bondage to God by ensuring his compliance with the Divine Law. In the capacity of the representative and messenger of God, prophets exercise God's political and legal sovereignty on earth. To obey the prophets is to comply with God's will. Referring to the authority of Muhammad, the Quran declares that: "whoso obeys the Messenger obeys Allah . . ."[15] According to the doctrine of *khalifah*, after the prophet the *ummah* as the vicegerent of God exercises authority. At this stage, the whole community is entitled to rule, Mawdudi asserted, because "it has not been stated [in the Quran] that any particular person or class among them will be raised to that position."[16]

This principle that entitles members of the *ummah* to leadership rule regardless of their family, clan and class affiliations has set the Sunni doctrine of *khalifah* apart from the Shi'i doctrine of *imamah*, and has caused major disputes within Sunnism itself. If the *ummah*, as the vicegerent of God, is reserved the right to manage its affairs in compliance with God's will, then the community is entitled to delegate communal leadership to anyone it chooses. Therefore, a caliph is a caliph because the *ummah* has delegated political authority to him. This delegation of authority—which is carried out by communal consultation (*shura*), consensus (*ijma*) and oath of allegiance (*bay'ah*)—gives the *khalifah* a semblance of democracy. According to Mawdudi, "popular vicegerency . . . forms the basis of democracy in an Islamic state . . . ,"[17] since its practical meaning is that the consent of all Muslims, or at least a majority of them, is necessary for the establishment and continuity of leadership.

While the Sunnis generally accept the basic premises of the doctrine of delegation, they are divided over the scope and nature of the doctrine of obligation. Those who take an orthodox position favor *ummah's* absolute obedience to authority and its total passivism. They reject any form of control over leaders because, in their view, absoluteness secures the most essential goals of the *ummah*—those being law and order. Preservation of law and order, according to some early supporters of this position, even justifies absolute obedience to unjust leaders. According to Ahmad ibn Tamiyyah, "Sixty days of an unjust ruler are much better than one night of lawlessness."[18] Later advocates of orthodoxy, however, rejected absolute obedience to unjust rule by asserting that obedience to injustice is un-Islamic, and thus unacceptable, because it makes *ummah* indifferent to political life.

Although this orthodox position bears a great similarity with some non-Islamic positions, it is indeed the Quran and *Hadith* that explicitly command the *ummah* to obey its leadership. Exegetists of the Quran profess that when the Quran says: "O you who believe! Obey Allah, and obey the messenger and those of you in authority . . ."[19] it is indeed commanding absolute obedience to the caliph. Muhammad is also believed to have said: "The Sultan [political authority] is the shadow of God on earth"[20] and, in this capacity, he should be obeyed.

The second position favors obedience to authority as long as authority rules on the basis of the Divine Law. The advocates of conditional obedience to authority reject obligatory passivism and affirm the *ummah's* right to disobey and oppose those leaders who do not comply with Islam. Qutb, who insisted that God and His representative on earth— the caliph—should be obeyed, clearly made obedience to the caliph conditional upon the caliph's compliance with the Divine Law and observance of communal interests. The *ummah*, he affirmed, is not obliged to follow a caliph who does not meet these conditions.[21] The Quran and *Hadith* command the majority of believers to disobey unjust leaders and to remove them by such peaceful means as *shura* and *ijma* if possible, and by force if necessary.

The doctrine of obligation, therefore, designates to the caliph certain obligations. The caliph is not only required to comply with Islam and rule in justice, he is also expected to pursue communal interests. In these pursuits, the caliph should consult with the *ummah* or a selected group from them. The Quran commanded Muhammad to ". . . consult with them [his companions] in the conduct of affairs [*umur*]. And when

you have decided on a course of action, place your trust in Allah."²²
Although the prophet frequently called for and followed his companions'
advice in political matters, it is not clear whether the Quran intended
to make it obligatory on the part of the caliph to follow the advice of
the community. Ali's tradition, and Muhammad's *Sunnah* and *Hadith*
affirm the caliph's obligation to follow advice. Muhammad believed that
the Quran meant to hold the caliph responsible for ". . . taking council
with knowledgeable people (*ahl ar-ra'ay*) and follow them therein."²³
This interpretation, however, limits the caliph's obligation to seek and
follow only the advice of a selected few—the elites—rather than the
community at large. This limitation not only applies to the actual day-
to-day management of communal affairs, but also to more crucial tasks
including the choice of a successor to the caliph. This elitist element of
the doctrine of *khalifah*, which grants the task of leadership to a selected
few, sets this doctrine apart from those democratic theories that acknowledge the role of the community at large.

The Caliph's Legitimacy

In the first chapter I suggested that the legitimacy matrix varies with
the type of polity. In developed and highly-institutionalized systems,
for instance, institutional features are the primary determinants of
legitimacy, while leadership characteristics most effectively explain legitimacy in developing systems. In the Islamic polity, as a non-institutionalized polity, leadership legitimacy determines the degree of legitimacy of the system and its policies. While the Islamic community
agrees on some basic sources of leadership legitimacy, there is no
consensus on the relative significance of these sources. These disputes
are reflected in the sectarian divisions over the doctrines of *khalifah* and
imamah. With varying interpretations, however, these doctrines attribute
legitimacy to leaders' personal qualities, performance and modes of
succession to power.

In the doctrine of *khalifah*, the leader is required to possess certain
physical, psychological/moral and social/philosophical qualities. Sunni
scholars have generally agreed that the caliph should be of sound mind
and body; he should also demonstrate justice, maturity, dedication,
courage, knowledge and competence in his role as the administrator of
communal affairs.²⁴ The doctrine is explicitly exclusive in the sense that
it disqualifies females and non-Qurayshites (i.e. non-Arabs) from performing leadership roles. Only males, who are capable and qualified,
may be chosen as the caliph.²⁵ Muhammad Rashid Rida, Abu Muhammad
Ali ibn Ahmad ibn Hazm, 'Abd al-Rahman ibn Muhammad ibn-Khaldun
and a host of other Muslim thinkers believe that the *khalifah* is the

exclusive right of the Quraysh family. This is intended to preserve the dominance of Arabs in the community and to ensure that the caliphs possess moral and psychological qualities that are inherent in the prophet's family. To assure Arabism in the doctrine of *khalifah*, Rida asserted, the caliph should be a Qurayshite ". . . in order to preserve the link with the 'geographical cradle of Islam, the Hijaz.'"[26] Non-Arabs, thus, should be denied leadership roles.

This doctrine's emphasis on familial ties with Muhammad—Qurayshite descendancy—did by no means intend to attach divinity to the caliph. Unlike the doctrines of *imamah*, the Sunnis originally ruled out any divine association between the caliphs and God. Muhammad and the early caliphs were simply known to be humans with superior qualities and made no claims to divinity. With the expansion of Islam, and in response to the sectarian and political ideals and realities of the time, the later caliphs gradually claimed divine association.

Another major source of the caliph's legitimacy is his ability to enforce Islamic laws and to effectively pursue communal interests. This, of course, entitles only those who believe in Islam and who are capable of interpreting the *Shari'ah* to the *khalifah*. If the purpose of the Islamic polity is the enforcement of the Divine Laws, rather than self-determination for a racial or cultural grouping, ". . . it is obvious that only a person who believes in the Divine origin of that Law—in a word, a Muslim—may be entrusted with the office of head of the state."[27] In Muhammad Asad's view, just as there can be no fully Islamic life without an Islamic state, no state can be termed truly Islamic unless it is administered by people who submit to the Islamic Divine Laws. This position excludes non-Muslims from the position of authority. It is logical to conclude that in the Islamic polity, which is an ideological polity charged with enforcing Islamic principles, only Muslims who are committed to upholding Islamic principles should be entrusted with the leadership role.

Belief in Islam is a necessary but not the only characteristic of the caliph. To administer the Divine Laws, the caliph should also be the most righteous, knowledgeable and capable administrator. The *ummah*'s acceptance of the caliph, Qutb asserted, is contingent upon his faithfulness to the *Shari'ah* as well as his aggressive pursuit of communal interests. The *ummah*'s obligation to follow the caliph ceases with the caliph's deviance from the *Shari'ah*, since the Quran insists that one who does not govern by God's revelation is a non-believer (*ka'far*) who should be disobeyed and fought by committed Muslims.[28]

The most controversial source of the caliph's legitimacy is the manner by which he is succeeded to the position of authority. This is a controversial issue because unlike the issues of the caliph's attributes and functions, about which the *Shari'ah* is specific, there is no particular mode of succession to the rule that is specifically laid down in the *Shari'ah*. This lack of specificity combined with the Quran's assertions about the community's participation in managing its affairs have made the Sunnis believe that the details of leadership succession ought ". . . to be devised by the community in accordance with its best interests and the exigencies of the time."[29] Leadership legitimacy, therefore, partly depends upon the community's meaningful input into decision-making about leadership succession. Theoretically, this participation is provided through communal consultation (*shura*), consensus (*ijma*) and oath of allegiance (*bay'ah*). However, neither the scope nor the mode of the *ummah*'s participation are specific in the Quran and the *Hadith*.

Defining the communal role broadly, Mawdudi supported an elective process for the choice of the caliph. He suggested, however, that the caliph's election should not involve self-nomination, competition and public campaign because these acts represent a degree of greed and self-aggrandizement on the part of the candidate. These attributes are incompatible with such qualities as submissiveness to God's absolute authority and self-worth which are necessary for the caliph. Mawdudi suggested that to avoid these problems in the election process, a public agency like an elections commissioner should be charged with identifying and publicizing qualified candidates.[30] Mawdudi's recommendations are not based on any specific *Shari'ah* rulings, rather it is up to the community to devise an acceptable method in the choice of the caliph to ensure his legitimacy.

The Caliph's Functions

Since in the Islamic state fusion or limited separation of powers are preferred to a radical separation of powers, the caliph's functions are by no means limited to just the execution of laws. While as the chief executive officer of the state the caliph is primarily in charge of implementing the divinely-ordained Islamic laws and administering communal affairs, his responsibilities also involve limited legislative and judicial functions. As in any other constitutional state where authorities' powers are limited, in the Islamic state the caliph's powers are limited to what has been specifically delegated to him by God—the ultimate sovereign—and his vicegerents—the *ummah*.

To maintain the Islamic nature of the state and to preserve the supremacy of God's will, the caliph must do his utmost to implement the *Shari'ah* which is the constitution of this state. Without a consistent application of these rulings, no true Islamic state exists. In implementing the *Shari'ah*, the caliph is charged with certain administrative, military, judicial, legislative and even religious tasks. Abul Hasan Ali ibn Muhammad al-Mawardi enumerated these tasks as follows:

> The defense and maintenance of religion, the decision of legal disputes, the protection of the territory of Islam, the punishment of wrong doers, the provision of troops for guarding the frontiers, the waging of *Jihad* ("holy war") against those who refuse to accept Islam or submit to Muslim rule, the organization and collection of taxes, the payment of salaries and the administration of public funds, the appointment of competent officials, and lastly, personal attention to the details of government.[31]

God, as the absolute sovereign, has ordained laws that are supreme in the Islamic state. Human legislation is permitted only to the degree that it is consistent with and assists in the implementation of the *Shari'ah*. Mawdudi, who asserted the supremacy of God's will as expressed in the *Shari'ah*, insisted that human laws that are inconsistent with the *Shari'ah* are not binding upon Muslims.[32] The caliph's legislative function is limited to the adoption of secondary laws and administrative rules necessary for the implementation of the *Shari'ah* and the management of communal affairs. This legislative responsibility is one that the caliph shares with a consultative council (*Majlis-i shura*). Although it is not clear whether the caliph is obliged to follow the advice of this council, he must seek their advice in adopting subordinate legislation.[33]

Even though Islam accounts for some degree of independence for the judiciary, the early caliphs exercised important judicial functions. However, later caliphs delegated most of their judicial function to independent judges (*qudat*).

A major distinction between the functions of the Sunni caliphs and the Shi'i imams is that while the Shi'i imams maintained their claims to both political and religious authority the Sunni caliphs gradually concentrated on temporal authority and avoided interfering in spiritual affairs. The early caliphs, especially the four Rightly-Guided ones, exercised political and spiritual authority. As temporal authority was separated from spiritual authority in the practice of *khalifah*, the later interpretations of the Sunni doctrine of *khalifah* barred the caliph from dispensing any spiritual instructions. As Ignaz Goldziher describes it, the caliph became nothing but the successor of the one who preceded him and, thus, maintained no special qualities to allow him to exercise any spiritual authority.[34]

Modes of Succession to Power

A principal sectarian dispute in Islam has revolved around the question of succession to the *khalifah*. As early as the time of Muhammad's death, the Shi'is recognized the prophet's right to appoint his successor and, by accepting the doctrine of appointment (*wisayah*), acknowledged Ali's and his progeny's rights to the *imamah* of the community. The Sunnis rejected the doctrine of appointment on the grounds that neither the Quran, *Sunnah* nor authentic *Hadith* had explicitly acknowledged Muhammad's responsibility for choosing his successor, nor did Muhammad intend to appoint Ali as the first caliph.

The Quran, according to the Sunni position, had avoided specific instructions in procedural matters, including succession to the prophet, simply because for the Quran to remain a universal book of guidance applicable at all times and to all people it only had to deal with matters relating to right and wrong or good and evil. Therefore, the Quran only stipulated that the most suitable person should be appointed the caliph,[35] and omitted any particular procedure for choosing him. This was intended to allow the community, Sunnis argue, to devise necessary methods for leadership succession in accordance with its requirements and needs. At different times and under different circumstances, the community might find different modes of succession appropriate, as evidenced by the different methods employed for the choice of the four Rightly-Guided Caliphs.

The community must employ the most appropriate method which would result in the choice of the most suitable person. In Mawdudi's view, the most suitable person not only possesses the necessary attributes, but is also able to secure the *ummah*'s confidence. According to him, to ensure the confidence and support of the *ummah*, the choice of the caliph should be based not only on the free will of the people but should also reflect a degree of egalitarianism by rejecting any monopolistic claims to the *khalifah* by any clans or class.[36] Mawdudi's recommendations, however, radically diverge from the mainstream Sunni thought and practice that advocate elitism in the choice of the leadership by limiting the popular role in this process and by designating the Quraysh family a primary, if not monopolistic, right to the *khalifah*.

The Sunni positions on the question of succession are founded upon three interrelated doctrines of *shura, ijma* and *bay'ah*, which are examined in detail in the following pages.

Doctrine of Consultation (Shura). The doctrine of *shura*, which enjoys widespread support among the Sunnis and includes some Shi'i advocates as well, basically refers to the Islamic belief in the right of the *ummah* to manage its affairs through mutual consultation. Ever since Muhammad's death, however, the *ummah* has been divided over the scope of this right. The Sunnis have generally acknowledged more extensive rights for the community than do the Shi'is. For instance, unlike the Shi'is who by advocating the doctrine of appointment (*wisayah*) generally deny the community a meaningful role in choosing its imam, the Sunnis believe that communal participation in this process through mutual consultation is explicitly accepted by Islam. The Sunnis find the authority of the doctrine of consultation in the practical necessities of the *ummah* and *khalifah*, the Quranic injunctions, and the prophet's *Hadith* and *Sunnah*.

From the Sunni perspective, popular participation and consent legitimize the authority of the caliph and subsequently enable him to rule more effectively due to his bond with the *ummah*. The Sunnis insist that the Quran has explicitly accepted communal right to consultation by contending that the believers' communal business is to be transacted in consultation among themselves. They suggest that the Quran also commanded Muhammad to consult the believers in managing their affairs.[37] Even though there is no consensus that these Quranic injunctions create an obligation on the part of the *ummah* to engage in consultation, they form the essential core of the Islamic approach to political life. On the basis of these Quranic injunctions, consultation is the most suitable instrument for the management of communal affairs unless the *Shari'ah* has ruled otherwise. Since the *Shari'ah* is silent on the specific modes of succession to power, it is up to the community to determine the manner by which the caliph is chosen.

Muhammad's authentic *Hadith*, according to the Sunnis, also affirm the authority of *shura*. Muhammad ibn Yazid ibn Maja has quoted the prophet saying: "Follow the largest group." Ahmad ibn Muhammad ibn Hanbal also suggested that Muhammad told his followers: "It is your duty to stand by the United Community and the majority [*al-ammah*]."[38] During his reign, Muhammad sought and followed the advice of his companions. This prophet's practice was not only based on the *Shari'ah* but also reflected the pre-Islamic Arab political practices. In the Arab tribal institution of *al-Nadawa*, which was a tribal council consisting of the elders of the tribe, communal affairs were decided upon by mutual consultation. However, *al-Nadawa* was an elitist arrangement whose membership consisted of leaders of the tribal families and whose function was to represent kinship groupings rather than the population at large.[39]

While it is suggested that the doctrine of *shura* was intended to disestablish the elitist nature of *al-Nadawa* by transforming tribal communalism into Islamic individualism, and thus, allowing for a meaningful popular participation in the deliberations of communal affairs, the practice of consultation even during the prophet's rule was limited to a selected few. Although the Quran and other *Shari'ah* sources never intended to limit participation in consultation to a particular group or class of the believers, the choice of the caliph was frequently made by the elites rather than the population at large.

Islamic Political Leadership

Advocates of the doctrine of *shura* insist that it, at least theoretically, justifies an elective process for the choice of the caliph. To them, this doctrine rules out any assumption of the *khalifah* through non-elective means. Succession to power through inheritance—which is common in monarchies—and other non-elective modes, thus, is ". . . automatically, even though the claimant be a Muslim, as illegal as an imposition of power from outside the Muslim community."[40] Islamic monarchies are un-Islamic regardless of their pretensions to religiosity because, as Pakistani Islamic historians concluded: ". . . there was no place for kingship in Islam and succession could not be on a hereditary basis. The community as a whole must have the right to choose its leader and the right to remove him."[41]

Although the doctrine of *shura* establishes the elective nature of the caliph's succession, the *Shari'ah* does not specify the method of election. Therefore, the *ummah* should determine the method of the caliph's election—direct or indirect, proportional or non-proportional, etc.—as long as these methods are consistent with the *Shari'ah*. Those who oppose a Western-style democratic election of the caliph involving nomination, campaign and general election contend that this method might not lead to the choice of the best person, as required by the Quran; does not establish a mutual obligation between the caliph and the *ummah*, since unlike *bay'ah* a vote does not have the force of bilateral agreement; and self-nomination and public campaigning disqualifies the individual, since a person who offers himself for the position of authority lacks submissiveness to God and abuses his position of trust and should be ignored.[42]

Supporters of a Western-style democratic procedure for the choice of the caliph argue that even though this method was not employed during the early caliphs, it is not specifically forbidden by the *Shari'ah*. However, the successful working of this method in the Islamic system primarily depends upon a conscientious electorate who, being aware of its rights and obligations under Islamic laws, is likely to choose the most appropriate person for leadership. In their view, the ability to choose the most suitable person also depends upon the community's awareness of the existence of qualified individuals and their willingness to serve as the caliph. Therefore, self-nomination and campaign are not inappropriate undertakings if the community is to be protected from appointing unsuitable individuals to the *khalifah*. Moreover, supporters of a democratic procedure insist that even though popular vote does not have a contractual power binding the *ummah* to the caliph, it is still an expression of the *ummah's* preference for a candidate whom they can remove from office or reject in the next election if he lacks competence. The ability to check the caliph's actions and to prevent him from setting aside the *Shari'ah* rules and interests of the community, according to Mawdudi, is the principal implication of the doctrine of *shura*.[43]

The majority of Shi'is oppose the doctrine of *shura* and any democratic procedures for the choice of the caliph on the grounds that they are neither founded on Islamic principles nor are they appropriate for the leadership of the community. According to Shariati, democracy as the underlying objective of the doctrine of *shura* ". . . is an anti-revolutionary regime that is incompatible with the ideological leadership of the society."[44] Furthermore, he asserted, the community could not have chosen a dynamic caliph without the prophet's involvement under the circumstances of fourteen centuries ago. However, the *Zaydiyyah* branch of Shi'ism that rejected the *khalifah* system accepted the doctrine of *shura* and, consequently, took the position that election is a suitable method for the choice of the imam.

Doctrine of Consensus (Ijma). In the Sunni political thought, *ijma* originally referred to the unanimous opinion of any generation of Muslims on a religious matter which would constitute an authority (*hujjah*) that ought to be accepted by future generations of Muslims.[45] However, since religious and political realms are not distinct in Islam, the Sunnis have applied this doctrine to political issues as well. Whereas *ijma*, like *shura*, became a doctrinal justification for the community's role in managing its affairs as the vicegerent of God, it did not devise any specific method for ascertaining the people's will.

Disagreements about sources of the authority, the essence as well as the scope of *ijma*, gradually clouded this doctrine in the Sunni thought. Serious questions that were raised about the authority of *ijma* led to the conclusion that ". . . there is no sound basis for the traditional doctrine of consensus in Islam."[46] However, since the basic premises of the original doctrine of *ijma* is intertwined with the Sunni doctrine of *shura*, an outright rejection of *ijma* seems to be logically incompatible with the democratic premises of the Sunni political thought. Furthermore, not only intellect (*'aql*) but also the Quran, *Sunnah, Hadith* and even pre-Islamic Arab practices justify the doctrine of *ijma*.

Ijma was originally introduced as a response to socio-political necessities, but gradually gained religious sanctions.[47] According to the Sunnis, as the Quran established the authority of *shura*, by asking the prophet to consult his community, it did indeed accept the authority of *ijma*. In other words, the doctrine of *shura* implicitly encompasses the essence of the doctrine of *ijma*. Muhammad also accepted *ijma* by professing that the *ummah* will never consent on a wrong course of action.[48] Moreover, according to al-Ghazali, Muhammad's tradition of seeking his companions' advice is the strongest proof for the authority of *ijma*.[49] The practice of *ijma* also dates back to the pre-Islamic Arab social values which generally encouraged adherence to communal consensus developed and handed down by previous generations.

The disputes over the essence and scope of *ijma* revolved around two issues: the degree of communal obligation to follow past consensus, and whether *ijma* is the consensus of the community at large or that of just a selected few. As to the first issue, some Sunnis accepted the absolute obligation of the community and rejected any suggestion that communal obligation to follow *ijma* is relative to time and place. Others challenged absoluteness and acknowledged the community's obligation to follow the *ijma* that best suits it. According to Kemal A. Faruki,

> . . . we must acknowledge, without hesitation, the correctness of past *ijma* of the community within its given time-space context, i.e., presence, and yet, at the same time, we are fully entitled, indeed obliged, to exert fresh *ijtihad* and come to fresh *ijma* rulings on the same problems, when necessary, within the changed presence, or time-space context, of the living community.[50]

While the doctrine of *shura* provided a strong justification for the original doctrine of *ijma* and theoretically continued to be understood as the consensus of the community at large, the practice of *shura* was limited to the elites and virtually paved the way for the redefinition of the doctrine of *ijma*. During Muhammad and his early successors, leaders' companions and the learned few gradually monopolized the role of consultants to the leader and consequently *ijma* became the consensus of the elites rather than the community at large. This development heightened the ulama's influence and gradually justified their claim to the leadership of the community. Furthermore, with this redefinition, *ijma* became a barrier to the institution of *shura* by rejecting the right of the community at large to participate in the consultation process. Supporters of original *ijma*—the consensus of the community at large—insisted that since *ijma* is intended to be the consensus of the community as a whole, the consensus of the learned is only a transitory measure for finding the will of the people rather than a replacement for it. Thus, the *ijma* of the learned must ultimately secure the people's consent.

Critiques of the original doctrine reject its essential assumption that whatever the community, or at least the majority within it, agree upon is right under all circumstances. Although the prophet's *Hadith* explicitly supports this assumption, Asad insists, it is entirely unjustified to assume that the community is right at all times. He, thus, advises the community not to ". . . substitute for the un-Islamic autocracy of our past centuries the equally un-Islamic concept of unrestricted sovereignty on the part of the community as a whole."[51] The Shi'is also repudiate the *ijma* of the community as a suitable method for choosing the caliph because they assume that it is possible for the agreement of the community to result in error. In Abu Nasr Farabi's view, the consensus of the community has not always coincided with truth and justice. In fact, *ijma* has at times been unable to protect laws and meet communal needs, and thus, has resulted in usurpation and injustice.[52] Shi'is, therefore, reject the *ijma* of the community because "On the supposition of the non-existence of one immune to sin, there is in *ijma* no convincing proof. Hence, *ijma* is unprofitable because of the possibility of error in every individual of them, and so in all of them."[53] Shariati opposed the use of communal consensus as a means of choosing the caliph because *ijma* is an instrument of democracy which, in his opinion, is a system incapable of meeting developing societies' needs, since it is designed to preserve the status quo and to prevent the much needed change in developing societies.[54]

The redefinition of *ijma* to the consensus of the learned—the ulama—not only gained the support of the Sunni and Shi'i opponents, but was also conducive to a much desired legitimacy and acceptance of another Islamic doctrine—the doctrine of *ijtihad* (independent judgement). According to this doctrine, to arrive at decisions that reflect the spirit and intent of the *Shari'ah*, the Islamic community needs the assistance of experts in Islamic jurisprudence. Therefore, in the absence of the prophet and caliphs, the ulama have the right to issue canonically permissible decisions. According to Rida, decision-making authority that is entrusted to the community by God should be exercised by those who possess knowledge and judgement.[55] Some Muslim scholars not only extended the function of *ijtihad* but also transformed it from the individual *ijtihad* to a collective *ijtihad* by suggesting that for decisions to reflect communal consensus, they should be made by a body of jurisprudents rather than individual ulama.[56] As the Shi'is rejected the doctrines of *shura* and *ijma* of the community at large and acknowledged the right of the ulama in making decisions for the community, they regarded *ijtihad* as one of the greatest principles of Alid Shi'ism. They believed *ijtihad* enables the society to respond to the changing legal, economic and social needs on the basis of the spirit, logic and orientations of Islam. Free *ijtihad*, according to Shariati, prevents Islam from remaining within stagnant frameworks and provides the necessary dynamism in its developmental process. Shariati, however, equated *ijtihad* with *taqlid* (imitation and following) in Alid Shi'ism. *Taqlid*, which in his view is a progressive principle that entails following the opinions of the learned, provides the community with unity, organization and leadership. Under the Safavid Shi'ism, however, both *ijtihad* and *taqlid* were transformed into blind obedience to the ulama and consequently lost their value as instruments of creative and dynamic Islamic response to societal needs and developments.[57]

Doctrine of Oath of Allegiance (Bay'ah). The concept of *bay'ah* in the Quran and other Islamic documents is a reference to the adoption of Islam. In the political theory of Sunnism, however, the doctrine of *bay'ah* refers to the community's obligation to confirm the nominee for the position of caliph. Even though *bay'ah*, like *shura* and *ijma*, is an acknowledgment of the community's right to contribute to the process of choosing the caliph, it does not presuppose any particular method. It only involves the approval of the nominee regardless of the method of his succession to power, be it election or appointment. Once chosen by the community at large or by the notables, *bay'ah* is rendered to the caliph. This lack of preoccupation with a particular method combined with Ali's request for the *bay'ah* of the Islamic community at the time of assuming power as the fourth Rightly-Guided Caliph have provided the doctrine of *bay'ah* with an impressive versatility that has not only preserved it as an integral component of the Sunni doctrine of *khalifah* but has also made it compatible with the Shi'i doctrine of appointment (*wisayah*).

The Quran treats *bay'ah* as a contract between two consenting parties, the community and nominee. This contract, without which the *khalifah* is never considered valid on legal grounds, constitutes mutual obligations for both parties. It obliges the community to render obedience to the caliph, and in return, requires the caliph to govern the community in accordance with the *Shari'ah* and communal needs and interests. Implicit in this doctrine, therefore, is the rejection of the orthodox Sunni position that underscored the absolute authority of the caliph. The doctrine of *bay'ah* clearly implies that the community's obedience to the caliph could cease with the caliph's disregard for his contractual obligation. Like in other contractual obligations, disputes between the caliph and the community should be resolved in the court of law and in accordance with the *Shari'ah*. If the peaceful resolution of conflict is impossible, the *ummah* or any of its members is entitled to rebel against the erring caliph and to replace him with another leader.[58]

While the doctrine of *bay'ah* played an important role in the Sunni doctrine of *khalifah*, the practice of *bay'ah* was neither based on the free consent of the community nor did it create an irrevocable obligation which was meant to be in force during the lifetime of the caliph. In practice, to secure the *bay'ah* of the community, many nominees for the *khalifah* resorted to such means as bribery, intimidation and coercion. Whenever these means failed, the use of force was the general means for gaining the *bay'ah* of the community.

Doctrines of *Imamah*

Although with the gradual evolution of Shi'ism into a complex religio-political movement the Sunni-Shi'i polemic involved fundamental theological issues, the question of authority remained the central element of sectarian schism in Islam. Unlike the Sunnis, who by espousing the doctrine of *khalifah* arranged for permanent leadership of the community, the Shi'is devised instead various doctrines of *imamah* which, despite their explicit acknowledgment of the need for authority at all times, did not lay down a pragmatic foundation for permanent leadership of the community. While the Shi'is accepted and followed Ali and his progeny as the legitimate leaders, they failed to develop any specific explanation regarding leadership in the absence of the last imam. Initially, many oppositionist and revolutionary Shi'is rejected any form of authority other than that of the Hidden Imam—Mahdi. Recognizing the indispensability of uninterrupted leadership in the absence of Mahdi, later traditionalist and reformist custodians of Shi'ism developed explanations as to who the legitimate representative of the Imam should be and what should constitute his functions.[59] For instance, Khomeini's doctrine of *vilayat-i faqih*, which has not mustered much enthusiasm and support among Shi'i scholars, is an attempt to provide a framework for leadership in the absence of the Imam by suggesting that until Mahdi's return the ulama are the most qualified group of believers to govern the day-to-day affairs of the community.

The Shi'i doctrines of *imamah* are neither monolithic nor do they correspond to the practice of leadership in Islam. While the Shi'is advocated a plurality of the doctrines of *imamah* that culminated in the fragmentation of the Shi'i community, these doctrines shared in their basic elements. Despite these commonalities, and mostly due to political circumstances, doctrines of *imamah* did not in many respects correspond to the actual practice of political leadership in Islam. With the exception of Ali, the Shi'i imams were mainly considered the spiritual leaders of the community and were denied any leadership role in temporal affairs. Unlike the Sunnis who successfully adapted the doctrine of *khalifah* to the practical necessities of political life (which ironically brought the practice of *khalifah* close to some Shi'i leadership doctrines), the Shi'i jurists resisted adaptation of their *imamah* doctrines to the practice of leadership, and consequently, widened the gap between theory and practice.

As discussed earlier, the concept of imam in Sunni Islam is a reference either to a person who leads congregational prayers or, if the term is used as a synonym to caliph, to the political leaders of the community. *Imamah* in Sunnism is, therefore, either religious or political leadership of the community. In Shi'ism, the title of imam is essentially conferred on Ali and his legitimate Qurayshite successors. Although Shi'i Arabs, especially Iraqi Shi'is, have equated the concept of imam to that of Ayatullah (the highest-ranking clergy), the majority of *Ithna 'Ashari* Shi'is, especially Iranian Shi'is, have reserved this title for their twelve imams. Some Twelver thinkers, however, have attempted to broaden the concept of imam and apply it to the leaders of the community in general. Both Khomeini and Shariati used this concept as an equivalent to the Weberian notion of charismatic authority. Muhammad Husayn Tabataba'i also used the title of imam for ". . . a person who takes the lead in a community in a particular social movement or political ideology or scientific or religious form of thought."[60] This broad application of the concept has elicited enormous resistance by the community and other Shi'i scholars. In criticizing the use of the title of imam for Khomeini in the Islamic Republic of Iran, Muhammad Kadem Shariatmadari—a prominent Ayatullah—warned that acquiescence in the face of such a usage is blasphemous.[61] Therefore, under intense pressure, the Iranian leaders returned to the traditional practice of conferring the title of imam only on their twelve imams and designated Khomeini the title of *nayib-i imam* (imam's deputy).

In Shi'ism, where the fusion of religious and temporal authority is explicitly advocated, *imamah* is a reference to the dynamic religio-political leadership of the community by truthful, knowledgeable and infallible successors to the prophet. As discussed in the previous chapter, the Shi'i doctrines of *imamah* have their roots in the Quran and a host of Muhammad's *Sunnah* and *hadiths* including *Ghadir, Safinah, Thaqalayan, Manzilah* and *Haqq* as well as non-Islamic thought and traditions. This plurality of sources culminated in not only the support for divergent— and at times opposing—doctrines of *imamah* but also the development and predominance of those *imamah* doctrines that substantially differed from the initial Shi'i doctrine of leadership and the Sunni doctrine of *khalifah*. Although these doctrines varied in their interpretations of the attributes and roles of imams, they generally stressed the need for permanency of leadership, the *wisayah* process as a means of succession to power, *'ilm* (knowledge) and *ismah* (infallibility and sinlessness) of the imam, the redemptive nature of the imams' sufferings and death and occultation of the Imam.

According to the Shi'i doctrines, *imamah* is necessary for the preservation of order in the society and the pursuit of communal interests in accordance with the *Shari'ah*. Without leadership, the community may fall victim to disorder and confusion and ultimately might cease to subsist. "*Ummah* cannot exist without *imamah*," Shariati asserted.[62] Similarly, Tabataba'i suggested that "human society can never be without the figure whom Shi'ism calls the Imam whether or not he is recognized and known."[63] In the *Ithna 'Ashari* Shi'i thought, the indispensability of *imamah* is tied to the link between exoteric (*zahiri*) and esoteric (*batini*) aspects of religion. In this perspective, which is similar to the Sufi view, the esoteric and exoteric aspects of religion are intertwined to a point that neither the exoteric could exist without the esoteric, nor could esoteric be objectivized and revealed without the exoteric. As mediators between man and God, the prophet and imams realize the inner meaning of religion (esoteric) and reveal it to the believers. However, the prophet who initially brings the world of God can leave this world, but the earth can never be devoid of the imam, be him present or hidden, whose responsibility is to continue the prophet's functions of sustaining and interpreting the inner meanings of the religion.[64] Even if the imam is in hiding, the Hidden Imam's light and warmth, Shi'is argue, provide for the uninterrupted leadership of the community.

The Quran, Muhammad's *Hadith*, imams' *Ravayah* (sayings) and their *Sunnah* also assert the need for the permanency of *imamah*. For instance, Muhammad al-Baqir—the fifth imam—is reported as having said: "By God! God has not left the earth, since the death of Adam, without there being on it an Imam guiding [the people] to God. He is the proof of God to His servants and the earth will not remain without the proof of God to His servants."[65] Al-Baqir also found the necessity of prophecy and permanency of *imamah* in the Quran and *Hadith* by asserting that the Quran says: ". . . Allah will not chastise them [the people] while you [the prophet and imams] are among them . . ."[66] He insisted that the prophet also said: "The stars are safely for the people of the earth. If the stars went, there would come to the people of heaven, something hateful to them. And if the members of my family went, there would come to the people of earth, something hateful to them."[67] Muhammad ensured the continuation of leadership by appointing a ruler, in the shortest time possible, over territories which fell into Muslim hands.

The goal of permanency of *imamah* can only be realized if the imams were to be appointed to the position of authority. With minor exceptions, all Shi'i sects profess that it is the imam's responsibility to formally appoint his successor. In the *Ithna 'Ashari* doctrine of *imamah*, which was expounded upon by imam Ja'far as-Sadiq and gradually gained widespread support, a fundamental principle of *imamah* is designation (*nass*). The *imamah* is a prerogative bestowed by God upon a chosen person from the family of the prophet who, before his death and with God's guidance, transfers the *imamah* to another member of the prophet's family by an explicit designation (*nass*). Since the imam is chosen by God, the *ummah* has to acknowledge his leadership and obey his orders. As-Sadiq is believed to have said: "Whoever dies without having known and acknowledged the Imam of his time dies as an infidel."[68] The Quran also ordains the *ummah* to obey the imam.[69]

By limiting the choice of the imams to the prophet's family, the Shi'is intend to ensure that their imam possess superior qualities. While the Shi'is generally agree that their imams should be divinely-inspired possessors of religious knowledge (*'ilm*) who can authoritatively guide the community, they disagree on imams' personal attributes. According to the doctrine of *ismah* (sinlessness and infallibility), the Shi'i imams are immune from sin and error. The Quran insists that the imams are those from whom "God has removed all impurity and made them absolutely pure."[70] Shi'is claim Ali was appointed by Muhammad to lead the Muslim community for his exceptional attributes, his superior knowledge and infallibility, which he inherited as a member of the Quraysh family.

The doctrine of *ismah* has been the subject of intense controversies, especially in the light of the developments of *imamah* in Ithna 'Ashari Shi'ism. By proclaiming Muhammad and the imams to be *ma'sum*, the Shi'is did not initially mean to attach any form of divinity to their leaders. To them, sinlessness and infallibility were bestowed upon the imams by God's grace—God who is the one Lord, the Omnipotent and the Omniscient. According to this doctrine, which might have been formulated by the Shi'i ulama to establish the superiority of their imams over the Sunni caliphs,[71] imams possessed these qualities as a result of being an extension of the personality of the prophet. With the advent of Safavid Shi'ism, however, *imamah* was gradually transformed into the leadership of individuals with divine qualities who could not commit sin due to their physical/biological and psychological characteristics. As Goldziher suggests:

> The attributes ascribed to the souls of the *Imams* elevate them above the measure of human nature. The Imams are . . . 'free of evil impulses.' Sin cannot come near them; the substance of divine light that lodges in them could not be reconciled with sinful inclinations. Moreover, it also confers on them the highest degree of certain knowledge, complete infallibility.[72]

This development, which designated the imams of Safavid Shi'ism as unique metaphysical creatures who were naturally different from and superior to the Muslims, adversely affected the effectiveness of the imams as leaders of the community since Muslims could not identify with them. Furthermore, this development culminated in the growing gap between the two doctrines of *khalifah* and *imamah*. In sharp contrast to the Safavid Shi'i doctrine of *imamah*, the Sunnis did not attach any divinity to their caliphs. The Sunnis were also much less dogmatic than the Shi'is in attributing *ismah* to the prophet himself. While they generally agreed that Muhammad was immune from grave and trivial sins, they considered him to be a superior human being whose ". . . prophetic office was based on election to interpret the divine will, not on his personal aptitude; he did not bring to his prophethood intellectual advantages that raised him above the level of human knowledge."[73]

Another controversial component of the Shi'i, especially *Ithna 'Ashari*, doctrines of *imamah* is the belief in the redemptive nature of the imams' sufferings and death. Being deprived of political power and perceiving themselves as victims of Sunni oppressive and illegitimate rule, the Shi'is pursued either a quietist and compromising approach or an active oppositionist approach to authority. The majority of Shi'is accepted the doctrine of *taqiyyah* (dissimulation) which, due to the possibility of retaliation by the Sunni caliphs, underscored the need for concealment and quietism for the protection of Shi'ism and its followers. At the same time, the Shi'is praised their imams', particularly Husayn's, opposition to and confrontation with the Sunni caliphs and symbolized imams' defeat and martyrdom as a manifestation of their ultimate elevation to a higher existence. The Twelvers' colorful ceremonies such as *ta'ziyah* (passion play) and rituals involving self-flagellation (*sine zani* and *zanjir zani*, etc.) during the holy month of *Muharram*, especially on the tenth day of the month—*'Ashura*—when Husayn and his companions were annihilated, manifest both aspects of the Shi'i attitude. One being an expression of sorrow for being the victims of the powerful majority, and another being praise for revolt against oppression.

Many of these ceremonies were initiated during the Safavids (1501-1722 A.D.) and, by gaining official sanction, gradually became an integral component of Safavid Shi'ism. By incorporating the Persian and Christian— particularly the Western, and sixteenth and seventeenth centuries Eastern European—customs and traditions into those ceremonies, the Safavids made sure that the Shi'i rituals reflect the deep-rooted division between Safavid Shi'ism and Sunnism of the caliphs. The Shi'is' opposition to these rituals and the *imamah* of Safavid Shi'ism are mainly due to these rituals' efforts to underscore the compromising nature of the imams and downgrade their revolutionary stance. As Shariati suggested, Safavid Shi'ism and its rituals portrayed the imams as a group of oppressed, weak, cowardly, isolated and compromising individuals who were opposite to the Alid Shi'i imams who symbolized righteousness, strength, justice, knowledge, and opposition to ignorance and oppression.[74]

As noted in the previous chapter, differences of opinion in the Shi'i community over the issue of the choice of Ali's line as the legitimate successor to the prophet and Ali culminated in the fragmentation of the community. This fragmentation, which started soon after Ali, gradually intensified and produced numerous factions which differed not only in the number of imams and their lines of succession, but also in the imams' attributes and modes of succession to power. While most of these factions have vanished, at least the three factions of *Ithna 'Ashari* Shi'ism, *Zaydiyyah* and *Ismailiyyah* still follow distinct *imamah* doctrines and maintain important followings.

Imamah *in* Ithna 'Ashari *("Twelver") Shi'ism.* In the Twelver doctrine of *imamah*, the imam's leadership is an extension of Muhammad's prophecy—which as the Quran states, is the seal of prophecy[75]—". . . carrying on its [prophecy's] function except in the matter of divine inspiration without a mediator . . ."[76] This Shi'i attempt to equate the imam's status to that of the prophet is explained not only by the imams' attributes, which are similar to those of the prophet's except for his ability to receive divine ordinance, but also by intellect (*'aql*) that does not refute the imams' fitness for prophecy. "It is divine law that forbade our imams being given the name of prophecy, not reason, [for reason] does not forbid it."[77] Equating the imam's status with that of the prophet in the *Ithna 'Ashari* jurisprudence unites the authority of the *Shari'ah* with that of the imam, and consequently, makes the Twelver imam ". . . the living entity of the infallible divine law, its interpreter-maker and executor."[78] It is for the very same reason that the Twelvers rely on collections of imams' sayings (*Ravayah*), including Ali's *Nahj al-Balaghah* and the *Usul al-Kafi*, which as a continuation of the *Hadith* collections compose an essential source of the *Shari'ah*.

Assuming that only the progeny of Ali and Fatimah (Muhammad's daughter and Ali's wife) possess the necessary qualifications for *imamah*, the Twelvers followed Husayn's line and ended their *imamah* with Mahdi—the twelfth imam. Mahdi's *imamah*, according to them, continues until the day of return (*qiyamah*) when Mahdi will revolt against all injustices and sins, and will bring justice and prosperity to this world. Until the day of return, Mahdi remains occulted while his light and leadership guide the community in managing its affairs.

The doctrine of occultation (*ghaybah*) is the central element of the Twelver doctrine of *imamah*, and nicely corresponds to the Shi'i system of thought because Shi'ism has been the religion of protest and revolt from the outset. However, messianism—the belief in the return of a person who is the savior of humankind—is neither novel nor is it limited to the *Ithna 'Asharis* or even Muslims. All major ancient and modern religions and messianic political movements have in some form advocated the idea of occultation and have awaited the return of their occulted heros. Christianity, Judaism, Islam, Hinduism, Buddhism and Zoroastrianism whose followers were subjected to oppressive rules, at one time or another, cherished their messianic traditions.[79] Much before Islam,

Ethiopian Christians developed doctrines of return and reincarnation and still await the return of their messianic King Theodoros. Similar beliefs exist among Monguls and Muslims of Caucus who believe that their past heroic leaders will someday return and free them from oppression and injustice.

Muhammad's *Hadith* explicitly justify Islamic messianism. The prophet is believed to have said: "If there were to remain in the life of the world but one day, God would prolong that day until He sends in it a man from my community and my household. His name will be the same as my name. He will fill the earth with equity and justice as it was filled with oppression and tyranny."[80] A host of other *hadiths* also refer to Mahdi whose return will enable the humanity to reach perfection and full realization of spiritual life. Both Shi'ism and Sunnism accept Islamic messianism. However, while the identity of the Messiah is known in Shi'ism, neither in the Sunni nor in many other messianic movements is the identity of the Messiah known.

The Shi'i, especially the *Ithna 'Ashari*, doctrine of occultation was developed out of a need to underscore the permanency of *imamah*, even if it meant concealed rather than visible leadership of the community, to protect Mahdi in the face of the brutality of the political establishment and to give hope to the Shi'is that someday the oppression of the Sunni caliphs will end. The political establishment supported this doctrine. By declaring the end of succession to *imamah* and transferring the twelfth imam to a supernatural realm, the doctrine of occultation removed the imams' claims to temporal authority and culminated in a trend toward political quietism.[81] The Twelvers, who believed that no one but Ali and his progeny through Husayn had a legitimate claim to the *imamah*, denied the divine ordinance of any authority exercised by a human being during Mahdi's occultation. This did not mean, however, that the Twelver doctrine accepted the secularization of authority during the major occultation (940-   ), since it continued to require the authority to rule on the basis of the *Shari'ah* and Islamic principles in this period.

Imamah *in* Zaydiyyah. As in other Shi'i sects, *Zaydiyyah* prefers the doctrine of *imamah* to that of *khalifah*. However, the *Zaydis'* doctrine of *imamah*, which differs from those of the majority of Shi'is in terms of the Alid's line of *imamah* and the imam's mode of succession to power, somewhat resembles to and is tolerant of the Sunni doctrine and practice of *khalifah*. According to the *Zaydi* doctrine, *imamah* belongs to any descendants of Ali and his wife Fatimah who possess superior moral qualities and knowledge, and who is willing to rise and claim the leadership of the community.[82] The *Zaydis* followed Zayd ibn Ali, a great-grandson of Husayn, as their fifth imam, and ended their line of *imamah* with Mahdi. However, despite their lack of concurrence with the *khalifah*, the *Zaydis* made a great concession to the early caliphs by developing the theory of *imamate al-mafdul*—which maintained that it was possible for a man of lesser excellence to be appointed imam during the lifetime of a greater excellence. Consequently, they accepted the authority of Muhammad's companions to choose a successor to the prophet. Therefore, the *Zaydis* never made a rigid commitment to the appointive process. Instead, they maintained that communal consent is a source of legitimacy of *imamah*, and thus, favored an elective process for the choice of the imam.[83] Of course, this complicated the succession process in *Zaydiyyah* and culminated in rebellions and many claims to *imamah* after Zayd.

Imamah *in* Ismailiyyah. The *Ismaili* doctrine of *imamah* represents probably the most revolutionary twist in the concept and philosophy of leadership in Islam. It redefines the notion of Islamic prophecy and the historical roles of the prophet and his successors. This doctrine, like the *Ithna 'Ashari* doctrine of *imamah*, accepted the appointive process for leadership succession. However, it differed from other doctrines in its line of *imamah* and the status of its imams. The *Ismailis* followed Ismail—the son of the sixth imam Ja'far as-Sadiq—and his son Muhammad, and thereafter a series of occulted imams the last of whom, Ubayd Allah, reappeared as Mahdi. In the *Ismaili* political doctrine, which more than any other Islamic doctrine was influenced by neo-Platonic thought, the imam was elevated to a position equivalent or superior to that of prophecy. By assuming that divine revelation does not end with Muhammad's prophecy, the *Ismailis* concluded that: "With the same cyclical regularity, the seventh *natiq* is followed by the Mahdi, who, as an even more perfect manifestation of the Universal Intellect, is destined to pass beyond the work of his predecessors, including that of the prophet Muhammad."[84] This interpretation of the role of the imam is contrary to the Quranic declaration that Muhammad, as the seal of the prophets, has brought God's last message to humankind. Unlike the *Ithna 'Asharis*, who believed that imams including Mahdi are merely the interpreters of the inner meanings of Divine Laws brought by Muhammad, the *Ismailis* attached divinity to their imams. As Sami N. Makarem asserts: ". . . the Imam to the Ismailis is God manifested. He is the word of God and His Will, he is one of the three hypostases which constitute one undivided essence of God. . . . He is consequently higher than the prophet." The prophet, in this view, is inferior to the imam since he ". . . is the one who delivers the word of God, while the Imam . . . is the word of God itself."[85] This makes the *Ismaili* imam not only the messenger and executor but also the source of the Divine Law.

The *Ismaili* interpretation of the prophecy and *imamah* questions some of the most fundamental principles of Islam including the essence of Muhammad's prophecy and his message. This has resulted in the loss of the significance of some of these principles and has further fragmented the community over the question of authority in Islam.

The Imam's Legitimacy

According to mainstream doctrines of *imamah*, the imam's legitimacy is directly linked to his superior human attributes—the attributes that derive from his Qurayshite descendancy and enable him to understand the esoteric meanings of the *Shari'ah*—and to his capacity to identify the goals of the community and to guide it towards these goals in accordance with the divine ordinance. The sources of the imam's legitimacy can easily be distinguished from those of the caliph's since, unlike the caliph, the imam must possess qualities that can only be achieved through Qurayshite descendancy and Muhammad's lineage. To ensure that the imam possesses superior human qualities necessary for the *imamah* of the community, his succession to power should be based upon appointment by the ruling imam rather than communal consent. Therefore, generally speaking, the legitimacy of the imam is not dependent upon popular consent to his rule, rather it is the result of his designation to the position by God through the ruling imam. Furthermore, the imam's legitimacy depends upon his functions, the scope of which is much broader than that of the caliph's. While the caliph is primarily a temporal ruler, the Shi'i imam is theoretically both the temporal and religious leader whose effectiveness depends upon his familiarity with the inner meanings of the *Shari'ah* and his compliance with the divine ordinance. In view of the fact that imams were denied temporal authority and essentially performed a religious leadership role in the community, their legitimacy was linked primarily to their religious rather than political roles. However, many Shi'is attach a unique importance to the imams' political role and insist that their legitimacy also depends upon their revolutionary approach to the leadership of the community.

The legitimacy of Ali, the first Shi'i imam, is partly attributed to his ideal human qualities which include justice, flexibility, commitment, thoughtfulness, familiarity with the Quran and an "Islamic consciousness."[86] His Qurayshite descendancy and his opportunity to benefit from Muhammad's teachings, Shi'is assert, were also instrumental in making him an ideal imam. Furthermore, from the Shi'i viewpoint, Ali's *imamah* was the only legitimate leadership of the community because he was designated to this position by God through His prophet Muhammad.

The Imam's Functions

Unlike the Sunni caliph, who is merely a ruler, the Shi'i imam is theoretically charged with the dual function of political and religious leadership of the community. *Imamah* is, therefore, the religio-political leadership of the community by a person who, thanks to his personal attributes, must manage communal affairs and also must educate and guide his followers in accordance with the spirit of divine ordinance and with their individual and communal needs. As a religious leader, the imam interprets the inner meanings of the *Shari'ah* for the community by relying on the Islamic teachings and traditions. As a political leader, according to the doctrine of *imamah*, the imam assumes legislative, executive and judicial responsibilities. In this capacity, however, his role is not limited to the protection of the community and facilitation of its convenience. *Imamah* also involves the introduction and adoption of progressive goals, and a just, dynamic and revolutionary leadership of the community towards them.[87]

Modes of Succession to Power

The most essential difference between the two doctrines of *imamah* and *khalifah* is the issue of succession to power, which has an enormous impact on other aspects of these doctrines. As discussed earlier, the doctrine of *khalifah* acknowledges the right of the community at large, or some of its segments, to have input into the choice of caliphs through *shura*, *ijma* and *bay'ah*. With minor exceptions, Shi'is reject a popular role in the choice of imams and insist upon legitimism: imams should be people of Muhammad's lineage—through his daughter Fatimah and her husband Ali—who are formally designated by God through the prophet and his successors to the *imamah*. Theoretically, according to the doctrines of *imamah*, as Muhammad appointed Ali to the *imamah*, so should every ruling imam take the responsibility of foreseeing by inspiration who among the Alids is divinely chosen to be his successor and of officially announcing that choice.

The Shi'is dismiss communal consensus as an instrument for the choice of the imam simply because it is, in their opinion, inconsistent with Muhammad's *Sunnah* and with the conditions and requirements of Muslim societies. Classic and contemporary opposition to a democratic mode of succession to power in traditional Muslim societies originates in the presumptions that the community cannot consent on the best person for the *imamah* and that democratic methods do not produce the dynamic and responsible leadership necessary for the development of these societies. To ensure the continuity of qualified and committed leadership, Shi'is argue, those individuals who possess a natural right to the *imamah* should be appointed to this position. The two interrelated doctrines of natural right and appointment (*wisayah*) theoretically explain this Shi'i view.

Doctrine of Natural Right. In the Shi'i political thought, *imamah* is not so much a position as it is a right and a characteristic bestowed upon some charismatic personalities by God. In this view, the legitimacy of the imam primarily derives from his personal attributes rather than the method by which he succeeds to the position of authority. Thus, according to Shariati, the dispute over such methods as election, appointment, inheritance, etc. is meaningless, because what matters is who is chosen rather than how he is chosen to the *imamah*.[88]

Although this doctrine is theoretically sound and consistent with the basic premises of the doctrine of *imamah*, it does not provide any practical tool for the choice of imam. Shariati's assertion that it is the community's responsibility to acknowledge the value and natural right of the imam and to submit to his leadership manifestly contradicts his rejection of the Sunnis' advocacy of communal input into the choice of leader. Moreover, any assumption of effective involvement by the community disregards the basic principles of the doctrine of appointment (*wisayah*).

Doctrine of Appointment (Wisayah). *Wisayah* is a reference to the process by which the prophet and his rightful successors formally designate the most qualified individuals as imams of the community. Since this designation is made in response to divine inspiration, the community is required to follow the designated imam. Shi'is insist that Muhammad appointed Ali to *imamah* with the intent to keep leadership in his family, and consequently, to ensure that the most qualified individuals hold the position of authority. This decision was not only Muhammad's right but also his responsibility because the *ummah* was incapable of making a decision of this magnitude. Following Muhammad's *Sunnah*, Shi'is conclude, all ruling imams have a similar right/responsibility to appoint their successors.

In practice, however, *wisayah* became a process of choosing imams through inheritance.[89] Many Shi'is, especially the Twelvers, accepted a system of succession in which the choice usually fell upon one of the incumbent imam's sons and often upon the eldest one. This method of succession through a pragmatic appointive process prevailed in many traditional societies, including Muslim, and gave the doctrine of *wisayah* a semblance of monarchism. *Wisayah*, pragmatically redefined and at least partly shaped by ancient Persian political thought, explained the success of Shi'ism in Iran. However, traditionalist as well as reformist Shi'is rejected this practical redefinition in which they clearly saw a contradiction between the theoretical doctrines of *wisayah* and hereditary royalty.

Contemporary Leadership Doctrines

With the major occultation of Mahdi and the end of his deputies' rule, the Shi'i community that had historically insisted on the continuity of leadership needed to devise leadership doctrines which would enable the community to manage its affairs in the absence of the Imam. In developing such doctrines, many Muslim scholars adopted elitist approaches like Khomeini's *vilayat-i faqih* and Shariati's leadership of the *rowshanfikran*. These doctrines split the Islamic community into two groups: those believers who should lead because they are knowledgeable, wise and just; and those who have to follow the first group because their capacity to independently understand Islam and to enforce its rules is limited. This social stratification essentially relies upon the degree of the believers' knowledge of Islam and communal affairs as well as their superior moral standing and personal commitment to the just enforcement of Islamic principles.

Intellectual Elitism: Philosophical Foundations

As noted earlier, non-Arab and non-Islamic traditions and institutions were instrumental in forming the direction of Islamic, particularly Shi'i, thought. Among such foreign influences was Greek philosophy, especially the neo-Platonic doctrine of emanation and the notion of universal intellect, which lent strong support to those *imamah* doctrines that attached divinity to the Shi'i imams and designated them as an intermediary between man and God. The Greek philosophy exerted a similar influence on the post-*imamah* doctrines of leadership. The contemporary intellectual elitist approaches in Shi'ism resemble the neo-Platonic thought that envisions the ideal society as one in which the most knowledgeable rules. Muslim intellectual elitists reject the argument set forth by orthodox theologians who insist that the application of pure logic to doctrinal issues is a violent innovation and thus un-Islamic.[90] Knowledge and intellect, Muslim elitists stress, are the most significant qualities of leaders. However, they are sharply divided over the question of what constitutes knowledge. Influenced by neo-Platonism, some believe this knowledge is nothing but philosophy and conclude that the leader is none but the philosopher-king. For example, distinguishing between the imam, who is the spiritual leader of the community, and the chief of the community (*rais al-awwal*), Farabi suggested that while the imam possesses divine wisdom the chief or leader maintains human wisdom or philosophy. The philosopher should rule, Farabi insisted, because philosophy is an indispensable tool for the preservation of the society and the management of its affairs. Perfect practical human wisdom—

philosophy—and superior physical and moral qualities enable the philosopher-king to explain the character of divine and natural beings to the elites and masses and to prescribe rewards and punishments.[91]

In order to make neo-Platonic theory, which calls for the leadership of philosopher-king, applicable to the Islamic society, philosophy has to gain recognition by Muslims as a legitimate source of knowledge and perfect wisdom. To achieve this, philosophy needs to adapt to the fundamental principles of Islam. This requires the Islamization of philosophy, as long as this process does not jeopardize the truth as seen by philosophy. A host of Muslim scholars did indeed feel that such an adaptation is possible. In applying the Platonic theory to Islam, Farabi's philosophy substituted the prophet or the imam for the philosopher-king of Plato's Republic, and the *Shari'ah* for the laws.[92] The Shaikhis, followers of the Shaikhi movement named after Shaikh Ahmad al-Ahsa'i, also believed that a perfect Shi'i should rule as an intermediary between mankind and Mahdi during his occultation. Influenced by the Shaikhis, Jamal ad-Din al-Afghani stressed a parallel idea that acknowledged the need of every generation of mankind to be guided by a philosopher.[93] Similarly, a host of anti democratic-pluralist Shi'i and Sunni reformers have rejected the idea of majority rule, and instead, have advocated the right of the learned few to rule. For instance, in reference to the Virtuous City (*Medinah al-Fadilah*), the nineteenth-century Iranian reformers took a Platonic stand by suggesting that leadership belongs to the perfect man—the philosopher-king. Many took a paternalistic attitude towards the people and, by advocating intellectual elitism, conceived of themselves as being a dedicated special category of Perfect Men devoted to the spread of a new revelation.[94] Mawdudi preferred the rule of the intellectual elites to that of the majority. Allal al-Fassi also suggested that: "To direct a nation, there must be an aristocracy of thought."[95]

Vilayat-i Faqih *(Leadership of the Jurisprudent)*

Vilayat-i faqih is an elitist doctrine since it acknowledges the reality and necessity of social stratification in the Islamic community on the basis of knowledge and virtue. According to this doctrine, the *ummah* consists of a minority of the virtuous and learned individuals (*fuqaha*) and a majority who do not possess superior personal qualities. Since the majority's knowledge of Islam is inadequate, they are incapable of grasping their individual and communal affairs. Therefore, the first group should assume leadership of the community because in the ideological Islamic state only the *fuqaha* possess the necessary qualifications for the leadership of the community: knowledge of Islam, superior virtue and commitment to the just and effective enforcement of Islamic principles.

The two concepts of *vilayat* and *faqih* are central to this doctrine. *Vilayat* is the Farsi equivalent to the Arabic and Quranic concept of *wilayah*. In the Quran, numerous references have been made to *wilayah* and *wali*. In its Quranic usage, *wali* has meant "protecting friends and relatives," God and His friends, Satan and his friends, non-believers and enemies of God, and "successor."[96] *Wilayah* is a reference to the exercise of one's absolute authority over others with or without their consent. This authority is, however, limited by the divine prescriptions and the rights of the community. The two concepts of *faqih* and *'alim* that have been interchangeably used in the Shi'i literature, especially in Khomeini's *Kashif al-Ghita*, are references to virtuous, reasonable and just Muslims who possess a considerable amount of knowledge of Islamic theology and the ability to understand all individual and communal matters.

Having these attributes, the *faqih's* role in the community is identical to that of a *qayyem* or *wasi* (protector of rights) who is in charge of protecting the rights of the minors.[97] As a trustee, Khomeini suggested, the *faqih's* task ". . . over an entire population is not different from that of the trustee over minors, except quantitatively."[98] This implies that the *fuqaha* are the sole true leaders of the community. Any leadership other than that of the *fuqaha*, Khomeini concluded, is subject to the *fuqaha* "and thus must rightly belong to them, not those who, due to their ignorance of the law, must follow the *fuqaha's* guidance."[99] Therefore, the *fuqaha* must exercise supervision over all the planning, executive and administrative affairs of the community.

This doctrine has been overwhelmingly rejected by the Sunnis and has had its own share of criticisms in some Shi'i circles. Those who have rejected this doctrine have done so on the grounds that it is a novel and impractical doctrine with questionable Islamic foundation. Khomeini's call for actual leadership by theologians is a novel idea because it is radically different from the historical role of the clergy who only occasionally interfered in socio-political affairs of the community. It is impractical since it does not set specific qualifications for the leaders nor procedures for their choice.

The Islamic foundation of the doctrine is questionable because the idea of leadership by theologians is neither found in the Quran, since there was no theologian at the time of the Quran's revelation, nor in the early Shi'i thought and practices. However, Khomeini relied on the Quran, the *Hadith, Sunnah* and intellect (*'aql*) to justify his doctrine. In his view, the Quranic *surahs* of *al-Ahzab* and *Nasa* establish the *fuqaha's* right to leadership.[100] Acknowledging that a textual demonstration of *Hadith* is not conclusively supportive of this doctrine, Khomeini believed that the prophet's tradition and sayings also indicate that theologians are the only legitimate successors to the Imam. He claimed that Muhammad stated: "All affairs that are in the domain of the responsibility of the prophet are also the responsibility of the theologians."[101] Muhammad, Khomeini stressed, was meant to appoint theologians to succeed him when he said: My successors are "those who come after me, transmit my *Hadith* and *Sunnah* and teach it to the people after me," and "the *fuqaha* are the trustees of the prophets . . . as long as they do not follow the Sultan."[102]

The Shi'i imams' sayings and traditions are essential Islamic sources of Khomeini's doctrine. According to Khomeini, the sixth imam of Shi'ism, Ja'far as-Sadiq, considered the ulama the inheritors of the prophet's knowledge and, consequently, his trustee and successor. In his view, both the seventh imam, Musa al-Kazim, and the eighth imam, Rida,[103] elevated the status of the clergy to that of an honest trustee eligible to lead the community. In addition to these sources, Khomeini contended, the rule by theologians is a logical consequence of the nature of Islam and its application to all facets of the Islamic community.[104]

The Shi'i Ecclesiastics and Political Leadership

Not all Muslims believe that the ulama are indispensable in the Islamic community. Even those who acknowledge the need for the ulama do not agree on the structure and functions of the clerical establishment. As believers in man's ability to communicate with his God without a need for mediation, the Sunnis have generally dismissed the idea of a professional mediator—the Islamic clergy. Whether favoring a theocracy or other forms of government, Sunni scholars have predominantly suggested that political leadership by the clergy is neither practical nor does it facilitate the establishment of a true Islamic system. Qutb, a Sunni revivalist, did not acknowledge the need for a professional clergy, and insisted that the clergy were the enemies of Islam since they were aware that Islam has no professional clergy. He suggested that: "If Islam were to rule, the first act would be to banish the indolent who do not work [but make] a living in the name of religion [i.e. professional clergy]." Therefore, Qutb explicitly rejected the ulama's claim to leadership by stating that: "The kingdom of God on earth will not be established when religious leaders supervise sovereignty on earth as was the case under the power of the church, nor by men who pontificate in the name of Gods as was the case under 'theocracy' or divine rule . . ."[105] Anti-elitism of other Sunni scholars has led them to a similar stand on this issue. To many, since as vicegerents of God on earth all men are equal, there is no justification for a religious hierarchy and the rule of the ulama. For instance, Mawdudi who favored a theocratic system insisted that Islamic theocracy is rule by the whole community rather than the theologians.[106] In his constitutional proposals, he even refused to grant the ulama the power to review and veto legislation.[107]

Shi'i Muslims have generally acknowledged the need for a mediator between God and His followers whose primary function is to interpret the laws and guide the society in a proper direction. But, the Shi'is have disagreed about the nature of the clerical establishment and its specific functions in the Islamic society. Khomeini and other supporters of the theory of *vilayat-i faqih* presume that a centralized ulama establishment is indispensible and call for the ulama's actual rule over the community. The centralization of power in the clerical establishment is a frequently debated and highly-contested issue in contemporary Shi'ism. Opponents of centralization have insisted that a hierarchical ulama establishment is neither practical nor is it sanctioned by Islam. According to Sayyid Murtada Jaza'iri, the search for "the most learned" clergy is inappropriate and inconclusive, since the complexity and breadth of Islamic jurisprudence make it impossible for any theologian to be learned in all religious matters.[108] Discussing the institution of *marja-i taqlid* (source of imitation) in Shi'ism, Mahmud Taliqani also affirmed the impossibility of identifying the most-learned clergy. In Taliqani's view, the decentralization of the ulama establishment is not only sanctioned by the Quran, but is also necessitated by the practical requirements of modern life which make it impossible for any single person to give answers to all complex questions. Both Jaza'iri and Taliqani preferred a decentralized collective leadership, in the form of a commission that coordinates the policies of the clergy, over a centralized clerical establishment.[109] Numerous traditionalist and reformist Shi'is have advocated a similar position. Shariatmadari, a traditionalist Shi'i clergyman, opposed the politicization of the clerical establishment, since it might bring discredit on them and on Islam, and rejected the concentration of power in the hands of any one person.[110]

Although the institutionalization of *marja-i taqlid* was conducive to a centralized clerical establishment in the eighteenth and nineteenth centuries, historical opposition to a hierarchical system has gradually de-routinized and decentralized the clerical establishment. The lack of a formal structure and of an established mode of upward mobility in the clerical establishment indicates a de-routinized system that relies on informality and charismatic modes of leadership. The Shi'i clerics in Iran are an excellent example of an establishment that depends on an informal hierarchy and mode of mobility. Here, the status of a clergyman depends upon his knowledge and piety, the reputation of his teachers and mentors and public recognition of his abilities rather than a predetermined formal system of ranking. This informality has decentralized the clerical establishment. Decentralization has, in turn, caused fragmentation of the clerical establishment on the one hand, and independence for individual clergymen on the other.[111]

The issue of the clergy's role in the Islamic society has always been a controversial and polarizing one. Historically speaking, the Shi'is have entertained a diversity of ideas on this issue. As manifested by the scholastic disputes among the three Shi'i schools of *Usuli*, *Akhbari* and *Shaikhi* during the eighteenth and early nineteenth centuries and the present day controversies about Khomeini's doctrine, some Shi'is have accepted a very limited role for the clergy, while others have designated the clergy as the sole legitimate leaders of the Islamic community. The fundamentalist *Akhbaris* considered the Quran and prophet's tradition sufficient guides for the community and independent judgement (*ijtihad*) by the ulama unsound. They insisted that the ulama's role should simply involve searching through Islamic sources for solutions to problems. They therefore opposed the idea of leadership by the ulama. In contrast, the *Usulis* favored the leadership of those ulama who, in their opinion, were capable of independent judgement and could function as an agent of Mahdi. While the *Shaikhis*, the followers of Ahmad al-Ahsa'i, persisted in the need for a charismatic leader, they rejected the ulama's right to pass independent judgement. However, the *Shaikhi* contributions to Shi'i charismatic messianism reinforced the *Usuli* position on the role of the ulama in the leadership of the Islamic community.[112]

In Iran, where these doctrinal disputes were closely linked to the conflicts between the ulama and the political establishment—the conflicts that arose from the ulama's challenge to monarchs' authority and the monarchs' attempts to assert their sovereignty over the community and the clergy—the idea of the theologians' right to lead the community gradually gained momentum with the success of the *Usulis* by the end of the eighteenth century and is still alive in the late twentieth century. Influenced by the *Usuli* thought, contemporary Shi'i theologians have acknowledged a greater political role for the ulama. For instance, Shaikh Fadlullah Nuri, an avid opponent of constitutionalism in Iran, asserted that: "During the [Greater] Occultation of the [Twelfth] Imam, may God hasten his happy ending [i.e. his return] *Wilayat* is within the capacity [only] of the specialists in *fiqh* and of the *mujtahids*, not of a certain grocer or draper."[113] Murtada Mutahhari, an ideologue of the Islamic revolution in Iran, advocated a similar role for the theologians in the Islamic community.[114] According to Khomeini, the existence of the clerical establishment and the clergy's control over all facets of the community are imperative for the establishment and maintenance of Islam and of the Islamic state. Khomeini equated the clergy with Islam by saying: "clergy ['*akhund*] means Islam . . ."[115] The indispensability of the clergy, he asserted, is due to its role as a provider of a content for Islam. "Islam without the clergy is an Islam without content . . ."[116] In Khomeini's view, thus, anti-clericalism is treason against Islam and its ideals by those who are intent on the destruction of Islam. The role of the clergy in the Islamic state is to spread Islamic principles and ethics, to guide the people towards them, and through its leadership ensure the followers' compliance with Islam.[117]

This expansive interpretation of the clergy's role is not shared by all Shi'i thinkers. For instance, Shariati who, like Khomeini, advocated an Islamic order did not believe in the leadership role of the ulama. In his view, Islam does not have any official clergy with inherent rights and powers. As an advocate of Islamic protestantism—a movement which intends to revitalize Islam as a dynamic socio-political force—Shariati believed that what the Islamic community needs is a dynamic leadership that is equipped to deal with the requirements of modern life. He insisted that the knowledge of *fiqh* is not sufficient for dealing with today's complex issues.[118] Thus, supporting the Platonic notion of philosopher-king, Shariati asserted that leadership belongs to *rowshanfikran* (committed and enlightened intellectuals) who—being believers or non-believers and pious or non-pious—have the necessary knowledge and commitment to rule. *Rowshanfikran*, he suggested, are the only ones who think independently and are able to relate to generations of Muslims and their modern issues and can give birth to new social movements.[119]

Shariati's anti-clericalism and reformism, which could be partly attributed to his fascination with mysticism, were the primary reasons why he opted for the leadership of the *rowshanfikran* rather than the *fuqaha*. Shariati, like many Iranians, was critical of the clergy's corruption, rigidity, intolerance and lack of vision. While he criticized the quietist, compromising and aristocratic attitude of the clerical establishment during the Safavids and Qajars and praised the virtue, knowledge and dynamism of the Alid clergy—whom he called "the intellectual proletariat"—he refused to grant the clergy any role other than that of teacher and scholar. He insisted that the clergy is not a vicegerent of the imam, because the imam has not appointed any vicegerent.[120]

The Vali-i Faqih's *Legitimacy*

The *vali-i faqih's* legitimacy, like those of the Sunni caliph and Shi'i imam, depends upon his qualifications, his ability to effectively manage communal affairs and the manner by which he succeeds to the leadership position. His personal qualifications include a superior knowledge of the Islamic world view and its practical application to contemporary individual and communal affairs, familiarity with the administration of the state, superior moral standing and the ability to capably deal with complex issues as they arise.[121] Knowledge of Islam and styles of management are necessary but partial qualifications, according to Khomeini. Since the legitimacy of the leader depends upon his just application of Islamic principles, it is imperative that the *vali* remains sinless and just and leads a humble life.[122]

All advocates of the *vali-i faqih*'s rule underscore the significance of the leader's ability to carry out his responsibilities in accordance with Islamic laws. Any leader who does not abide by Islamic principles, who establishes a dictatorial regime and adopts un-Islamic policies is not qualified to rule. Khomeini instructed the people to revolt against the despotic leader who follows a path that is inconsistent with Islam.[123]

The legitimacy of the leader also depends upon the manner by which he has succeeded to the position of authority, but neither Khomeini nor other Shi'i scholars have set any specific procedures for the choice of the *vali-i faqih*. In his early writings, Khomeini insisted that *vilayat* is a position that is solely inherited from the prophet.[124] Mostly in response to public pressure and in an attempt to attract more support for his doctrine, Khomeini admitted the need for communal consent in the choice of the *vali-i faqih* in his later writings and speeches. Since it was the people who made the Islamic Republic a reality, Khomeini stated, the legitimacy of this system and its leadership depends upon popular support.[125] He added, people bring their leaders to and keep them in power. If people withdraw their support, leaders will lose their power.[126] Therefore, he suggests, "We are subject to the people's decisions. We will obey whatever their decisions may be."[127]

Clearly, Khomeini did not mean to imply that the Islamic state is founded upon the principle of popular sovereignty nor did he intend to establish a democratic procedure for the choice of the *vali-i faqih*. This is evident in his call for a mandatory obedience to the *vali* and acceptance of his decisions.

The Vali-i Faqih's *Functions*

According to Khomeini, the *vali-i faqih* basically performs a supervisory function in the community similar to that of the prophet and imams. This function includes supervision over limited legislative as well as executive and judicial functions. Muhammad, Khomeini asserted, acknowledged this right for the *vali-i faqih* and the ulama establishment by saying that: "The just *fuqaha* are in charge of all matters which are within the jurisdiction of the prophet."[128] Since the Islamic state is based on fusion or limited separation of powers, the functions of the head of the state—the *vali-i faqih*—is encompassing. The *vali-i faqih*'s legislative function is limited to supervision over the adoption of supplementary laws because the *Shari'ah* is the essential legal framework of the state, and thus, there is no need for an expansive legislative function.

The primary and most extensive function of the *vali-i faqih* is supervision over the execution of Islamic laws and principles. In this capacity, Khomeini stressed, the *vali-i faqih's* responsibility is to ensure the enforcement of the Islamic principles, rather than to make laws, because only compliance with divine laws could guarantee justice, happiness and prosperity for humankind.[129]

The *Ravayah* delegate judicial function to the *fuqaha* who, due to their superior knowledge and moral qualities, are most qualified to determine whether the believer is in compliance with the *Shari'ah* and, if necessary, decide on punishment.[130] As the highest *faqih*, in Khomeini's view, the *vali-i faqih* has the supreme authority over this judicial function.

Modes of Succession to Power

As noted earlier, Khomeini did not specifically set a procedure for the choice of the *vali-i faqih*. However, he preferred meritocracy to ascriptiveness. Therefore, he theoretically accepted any procedure that results in the choice of the most competent *faqih*, and rejected any system that promotes favoritism and culminates in self-imposed autocracy.[131] According to Khomeini, the ulama should play a determining role in the choice of the *vali-i faqih*. This draws Khomeini's doctrine closer to the later interpretations of the doctrine of *ijma* in the *khalifah* and *imamah* doctrines, whereby a selected few are charged with choosing the leader. Even Shariati, who advocated the leadership of *rowshanfikran* and rejected Khomeini's doctrine, stressed the need for the ulama's consensus in the choice of the leader. In Shariati's view, the selection of the leader during the occultation of Mahdi should be the responsibility of the knowledgeable individuals rather than the masses, because the masses are unqualified and unworthy of electing the leader. He asserted:

> Reason dictates that those learned ones (*'ulama'*) who know who is the most learned and best specialist of this school of thought . . . choose. The people who rely on and follow their religious leaders naturally accept their choice of the Imam's deputy . . . The Imam, while in *ghaybat*, grants the enlightened, pure and religiously aware *'ulama'* the task of guiding the faithful till the advent of his manifestation. . . .[132]

Obviously, Khomeini's doctrine of *vilayat-i faqih* and Shariati's leadership of the *rowshanfikran* do not differ on the procedure by which the leader comes to power as much as on the attributes of the leader. While Khomeini's doctrine is exclusive, in the sense that it limits leadership to the clergy, Shariati's doctrine supports leadership by any enlightened intellectual, be he a clergyman or not.

The ambiguity about the mode of succession culminated in debates and disputes among the framers of the Constitution of the Islamic Republic of Iran. It is generally accepted, however, that a council of experts (*Majlis-i khebregan*), not the public at large, is entitled to choose Khomeini's successor.

PRAGMATISM IN POLITICAL LEADERSHIP

While the doctrines of leadership varied and essentially reflected the sectarian disputes, the practices of leadership in Sunnism and Shi'ism followed a similar set of pragmatic procedures and principles predominant in most traditional polities. Essentially, both the *khalifah* and *imamah* systems increasingly relied on charismatic personalities whose legitimacy depended upon their personal attributes and, more importantly, upon their appointive mode of leadership succession. This appointment process gradually resembled the ancient monarchic system of succession to power through inheritance, whereby the eldest son of the leader would automatically inherit the position of authority. This practice in the *khalifah* system brought the Sunni practice of leadership closer to some of the Shi'i doctrinal positions.

The *Khalifah* System

Muhammad was a charismatic leader accepted by the *ummah* not only for his divine appointment but also for his superior attributes and leadership ability. As a spiritual authority, Muhammad brought and explicated the essential premises of Islam to the people. As a temporal ruler, he laid the foundation of the Islamic state and ruled according to Islam. As a judge, he ensured compliance with the Islamic world view. Muhammad's leadership role in maintaining and expanding the Islamic ideology and community made it abundantly clear that the survival of Islam and the success and spread of its message require leaders who can effectively follow the prophet's path. Initial disputes within the *ummah* after Muhammad's demise made it apparent that the increasingly diverse Islamic community can never agree upon the issue of leadership. As elaborately discussed in the previous chapter, disputes over this issue gradually led to intense disintegrating sectarian schisms.

Early successors to the prophet, especially the four Rightly-Guided Caliphs (*Khulafa ar-Rashidin*), were patriarchal leaders whose functions were similar to Muhammad's except for his prophetic function. As spiritual and temporal authorities, they administered both religious and political affairs of the community. From the outset, however, the two questions of legitimacy and mode of succession to power were controversial. The choice of these caliphs did not substantially reflect the Sunni doctrine of *khalifah*, although certain premises of the doctrine were observed. The choice of Abu-Bakr as the first caliph and the support for his leadership by some segments of the *ummah* were due to his popularity and prestige, his close association with Muhammad, his contributions to Islam and clannish rivalries which made him a compromise candidate who was less threatening, and consequently, more acceptable to various Quraysh clans. The community was neither consulted nor was its consensus secured for Abu-Bakr's choice. A selected few, the chiefs of the *muhajirin* (Meccan companions of the prophet) and the *ansar* (those believers who joined the prophet in the city of Medina), who were present in Medina at the time of Muhammad's demise, simply chose Abu-Bakr to succeed the prophet. The choice of the succeeding caliphs were based on a similar disregard for the Sunni doctrines of *shura* and *ijma*. Only *bay'ah*, in the form of endorsement by the elites, was employed in the choice of these caliphs. Abu-Bakr appointed Umar as his successor and in doing so he neither consulted the community nor did he seek their consensus. He only sought the support of the chiefs of clans and advised the community to obey Umar's rule. To ensure the peaceful transition of authority and to deny Ali access to this position, Umar formed a six-member council of electors and, by setting specific instructions, charged them with the responsibility of choosing his successor from among themselves. As in the previous cases, this procedure, which culminated in the choice of Uthman as the third caliph, was neither democratic nor did it correspond to the Sunni doctrines of leadership nor even to the Arab tribal customs.[133] Ali was installed as the successor to Uthman by popular support. This support was due to a legitimist view by Ali's followers who believed that the *khalifah* should remain in the family of the prophet. While Ali sought communal consent to his rule through *bay'ah*, he himself never accepted an elective principle of succession.[134]

With the bureaucratization of the *khalifah* system during the Umayyads (661-750 A.D.) and its developments during the Abbasids (750-1258 A.D.) and Ottomans (early sixteenth to 1924 A.D.) patriarchal rule was gradually transformed into patrimonialism and, subsequently, charismatic leaders were replaced by patrimonial bureaucratic rulers. As the influence of Islam and the *khalifah* disseminated to other lands, Islamic patrimonialism was further consolidated and bureaucratized. Bureaucratic patrimonialism necessitated a practical and institutionalized procedure for the choice of leaders. In adopting such a procedure, the patrimonial caliphs borrowed from the Persian and Byzantine empires the hereditary principle of succession, which was predominantly practiced in traditional systems and conformed with the pre-Islamic Arab tribal customs.[135] For example, Mu'awiyyah, the founder of the Umayyad dynasty, rebutted the legitimist argument and suggested that the legitimacy of the caliph depends upon his personal power and strength, his administrative ability to effectively manage the community and his political and military capabilities to expand the empire and defend it against its enemies. He combined the hereditary principle of succession with *bay'ah* and sought the elites' support for the leadership of Yazid, his son, whom he appointed as his successor. This practice continued throughout the Umayyads and their successors, the Abbasids, and gave the practice of succession a semblance of democratic election. Furthermore, this procedure culminated in a succession arrangement called *wilayat al-ahd* (heir apparent), whereby the ruling caliph would nominate someone for succession before his demise and would seek *bay'ah* for the successor from the community or a selected few.

The Abbasids gradually transformed this relatively simple succession process into an elaborate and complex one consisting of nomination of the successor in the presence of witnesses and securing the *bay'ah* of the whole community. However, in this process hereditary succession precluded any free choice. The Abbasid caliphs used every means at their disposal including bribery and threat to secure the *bay'ah* for their successors. Later, Abbasids also revived the legitimist argument, probably under the influence of Persians, by favoring the idea that leaders should be linked to the family of the prophet. They suggested that their rule was legitimate since they believed that they had inherited the *khalifah* from Muhammad.

These practices sharply varied from the Sunni doctrine of *khalifah* since the caliphs did not meet the leadership requirements nor did they succeed to this position on the basis of popular consent. This development transformed these caliphs into imperial autocrats whose legitimacy depended upon their ability to come to power and to maintain their rule by force, if necessary.[136] Adapting theory to this practice, the Sunni jurists acknowledged force to be a source of the caliphs' legitimacy,[137] and the caliphs increasingly relied on their bureaucratic and military power to preserve their rules. Reliance on force, however, heightened the disputes over the caliphs' sources of legitimacy and intensified challenges to their rules. Thus, despite the orthodox principle of absolute obedience to the caliph, some of the caliphs were abdicated, and their successors were appointed by the military (around 869 A.D.).

Although the early caliphs often had to rely on the support of the public and elites in order to preserve the legitimacy of their rule, they usually ruled the Islamic community with absolute authority. The centralization of power during the four Rightly-Guided Caliphs, which was partly due to the caliphs' patriarchal rule and the homogeneity of the *ummah*, enabled them to perform absolute administrative, judicial and limited legislative functions. This clearly charged the early caliphs with religious and political authority. The bureaucratization of the *khalifah* system, the rapidly growing heterogeneity of the *ummah*—as a result of the spread of Islam to new territories—and the subsequent centrifugal tendencies in the Islamic empire gradually decentralized the powers of the caliphs. Decentralization of power increasingly lessened the caliphs' authority, and eventually culminated in the separation of political and religious authority. Unlike their predecessors, the Umayyads explicitly acknowledged the separation of religion and politics, primarily functioned as political leaders and left religious leadership to the imams and the ulama. The reduction in the caliphs' political role continued during the Abbasids. From the ninth century onwards, the caliphs gradually withdrew from public accessibility and ultimately became mere ceremonial figures.

Even during the heyday of the *khalifah* system, the caliphs' roles were primarily limited to administrative and judicial functions. They never performed a critical legislative function, since their legislative role only entailed the interpretation, codification and systematization of the Islamic rules based on the Quran, *Sunnah, ijma,* analogy (*qiyas*) and *Hadith*. The early caliphs were also charged with judicial responsibilities. However, these responsibilities were gradually delegated to a *qadi* (judge) who usually acted independently. With further bureaucratization of authority and the subsequent limited separation of powers, an extensive judiciary was established. This hierarchical structure that was led by a *qadi al-qudat* (chief justice) gradually became the sole judicial arm of the Islamic state.

This limited separation of powers combined with administrative and political decentralization of authority gave vent to numerous and effective disintegrating tendencies in the conquered Islamic territories. As a result, regions and demographic groupings that possessed independent status prior to conversion to Islam gradually reasserted themselves mainly under sectarian adhesions, and established their own political organizations.

The *Imamah* System

To the dismay of Ali and his followers, the elites opted for the leadership of Abu-Bakr and refused to transfer authority to Ali after Muhammad's demise. Ali's followers, who later came to be known as Shi'is, insisted on Ali's and his progeny's legitimate right to authority and continued to support the leadership of the imams rather than the Sunni caliphs. However, with the exception of Ali who ruled as the fourth Rightly-Guided Caliph, none of the Shi'i imams actually succeeded to the position of temporal authority. Nevertheless, the imams exerted a tremendous amount of spiritual and religious authority in the Shi'i community.

To ensure the rule of Ali and his descendants, the practice of *imamah* was based on the principle of hereditary succession from the outset. Ali's demand for the communal *bay'ah* at the time of his succession to rule did not change this legitimist approach to succession among the Shi'is. As noted earlier, not only did the Shi'i imams continue to normally appoint their eldest sons as their successors but also the caliphs practiced this appointive process while they gave it some semblance of democracy by seeking the communal *bay'ah*.

Hasan, Ali's son, was appointed the second imam based on Ali's will and secured communal *bay'ah*. Mu'awiyyah rejected Hasan's claim to temporal authority by suggesting that the community would be better served by him because he is more qualified than Hasan. Hasan is believed to have conceded to Mu'awiyyah after receiving assurances that Mu'awiyyah would not appoint a successor and Hasan and Ali's progeny would be allowed to regain their right to temporal authority after him. The consolidation of the Umayyads' political power adversely affected the Shi'is' influence and practically diminished their chances of establishing an effective *imamah* system that could rule politically as well as spiritually. Husayn, Hasan's brother and successor, did not continue his predecessor's quietist and compromising attitude. He insisted that authority, temporal and spiritual, belongs to the prophet's family and considered it the duty of the rightful successor to fight for his inherent right to authority. Husayn revolted against Yazid, Mu'awiyyah's son and successor, and his authority. His revolt not only added an activist dimension to Shi'ism but also immensely contributed to the consolidation of the Shi'i identity and its rapid spread. For these very reasons, students of Shi'ism have referred to Husayn's revolt against Yazid at Karbala and his death at the hands of the Umayyad forces on the tenth of Muharram as the event that "set the seal on official Shi'ism."[138]

After Husayn, the practice of hereditary succession to *imamah* continued but with increasing emphasis on blood ties to the prophet and his daughter, Fatimah, rather than Ali. At this time, the disputes over the rightful line of succession and the number of imams were initiated, and have continued throughout the history of Shi'ism. The majority of Shi'is followed Husayn's son, Ali Zayn al-Abidin (658-712/713 A.D.), whom they believed Husayn had appointed as his successor. The *Ithna 'Ashari* or *Imami* Shi'is, who constitute the largest Shi'i faction today, essentially followed this line of succession until the occultation of the twelfth imam. Their imams, who were normally appointed on the basis of the hereditary succession of the eldest son, include: Ali (619/621-661 A.D.), Hasan (624-669 A.D.), Husayn (626-680 A.D.), Ali Zayn al-Abidin (658-712/ 713 A.D.), Muhammad al-Baqir (676-732 to 743 A.D.), Ja'far as-Sadiq (699, 702 or 705-765 A.D.), Musa Kazim (737, 745 or 746-799 A.D.), Ali al-Rida (765-818 A.D.), Muhammad al-Taqi (810-835 A.D.), Ali al-Hadi (827 or 829-868 A.D.), Hasan al-Askari (844, 845 or 846-873 or 874 A.D.), and Muhammad al-Mahdi (868-). The minority continued the Alid line by following Ali's third son, Muhammad ibn Hanafiyyah, rather than Zayn al-Abidin. The Shi'is were further factionalized by following different imams in these divergent lines of *imamah*.

As noted earlier, none of these imams, with the exception of Ali, exercised temporal power. Some accepted their role as the religious and spiritual leaders of their communities and pursued a quietist and compromising attitude towards the caliphs. Others insisted on their legitimate right to temporal authority. Husayn, in particular, never recognized the right of the caliphs to temporal authority and revolted against Yazid, the ruling caliph. The legitimist argument was skillfully developed by the fifth imam, Muhammad al-Baqir, and has remained the nucleus of the Shi'i thought. Realizing the impossibility of the imams' temporal rule under the circumstances, Baqir's son and successor—Ja'far as-Sadiq—accepted the legitimist argument but put forward the idea that the *imamah* and *khalifah* should remain separate institutions until an imam can ascend to the position of temporal authority by God's will. In the meantime, he asserted, the caliphs should exercise temporal authority while the imams should remain the religious and spiritual leaders of their communities.

This position not only separated temporal authority from religious authority in Shi'ism, but also justified the quietist approach to temporal authority pursued by most previous Shi'i imams. From then on, Shi'is believed that it is unnecessary for the imam to exercise, or even claim, temporal authority if the circumstance do not allow him to do so.[139] This process of depoliticization of *Imami* Shi'ism reached its apex with the occultation of the twelfth imam, Mahdi, who had apparently died in his infancy. The practical doctrine of occultation enabled the Shi'i leaders to postpone the realization of the Shi'i claim to political power indefinitely. Furthermore, it reinforced the earlier position that temporal rule is not an indispensable function of the imam and, thus, accentuated the spiritual and religious functions of the imams.

Post-*Imamah* Leadership

The leadership of the Shi'i community during the minor occultation of Mahdi (873-940) was delegated to a series of four learned individuals who, as deputies (*vukala* or *nuwwab*) to the imam, were essentially charged with guiding the community and disseminating the imam's command. These leaders were not elected by the community, they were appointed. The first deputy, Uthman ibn Sa'id Umari, was appointed by Mahdi. He was succeeded by his son Muhammad ibn Uthman Umari. Then, Abul Qasim Husayn ibn Ruh Nawbakhti and after his death Ali ibn Muhammad Simmari served in this capacity. Simmari was the last of these deputies and did not designate a successor, observing that the choice of his successor is up to God.[140] This brought the period of minor occultation and deputation of Mahdi to a close and commenced the period of major occultation (*ghaybat-i kubra*) which, in the opinion of the Shi'is, will continue until Mahdi's return.

Although the Shi'is have essentially agreed that there is no *imamah* but that of Mahdi, they have generally acknowledged the need for some form of leadership in the absence of the imam. However, they have neither specifically defined the functions of these leaders nor have they established a set procedure for their choice. The confusion and power vacuum caused by this lack of consensus over the issue of leadership has historically opened the door for the ulama's claim to political authority on behalf of the Hidden Imam.

There is no consensus on what, if any, political role should be played by the ulama in the Islamic community. The scholastic dispute among the *Akhbaris*, *Usulis* and *Shaikhis* was an exemplary indicator of the persistent schisms among the Shi'is, ulama and laymen, over the political role of the ulama. In Safavid Iran, where the kings laid claims to the imam's vicegerency (*niyabah*) through alleged descendancy from the line of the eighth imam (Rida), religio-spiritual and political leaderships were merged into one and were performed by the monarchs. This trend revived the old idea of theocracy and gradually encouraged the ulama to insist on a leadership role for the clergy. The ulama's weakness, vulnerability and dependency on the Safavids initially prevented them from challenging the political supremacy of the Safavid monarchs. Nevertheless, they refrained from acknowledging these monarchs' religio-spiritual leadership.

Late during the Safavids, the consolidation of the ulama's power brought a new challenge to the political leaders and ended the period of coexistence between the religious and political establishments. With the fall of the Safavids, the subsequent chaos and instability that continued for a half century and with the growing Sunni influence in Iran, the role of the ulama temporarily declined. The revival of the *Usuli* school during the *Zandiyyah* (1750-1794 A.D.) and finally the establishment of the Qajar dynasty (1794-1925 A.D.) whose kings—despite giving homage to religious symbols and assuming the title of "Shadow of God on Earth"—neither claimed descendancy from any imam nor sought any religious sanctions for their rule, later increased the clerics' power and made them more assertive in their claim to political authority.

The growing fragmentation of the clerical establishment during the constitutional revolution (1905-1911 A.D.) and some clerics' attempt at transforming this predominantly secular-nationalist movement into a religious one, for the purpose of ensuring the clerics' domination in the post-revolutionary Iran, added more fuel to the fire of anti-clericalism and reinforced the growing secularist tendencies. The unpopular, extremely secular and anti-clerical policies of the Pahlavis (1925-1979 A.D.), particularly during the 1960s and 1970s, ultimately forced the ulama to take a more cohesive and harmonious stand against the established political order. The organizational strength, resourcefulness and leadership capability of this temporarily cohesive establishment were instrumental in mobilizing popular support and providing leadership for the highly-fragmented opposition groups, ensuring the end of monarchism in Iran. Not to everyone's surprise, Khomeini's leadership of the 1978 revolution was indeed the stepping stone in the reformulation of the clerics' role in the Iranian society and the restoration of their political influence. The incorporation of the intensely debated and controversial doctrine of *vilayat-i faqih* in the Iranian constitution provides a legal and political framework for the supreme role of the ulama in the post-monarchic Iran. In this constitution, which explicitly stipulates that sovereignty belongs to God (Article 56), the *faqih*—the highest-ranking clergy—is tasked with leading the community (Article 5). In this capacity, he is solely accountable to God and not to the people.[141]

The practice of *vilayat-i faqih* in today's Iran is impressively congruent with its doctrine. At least from a functional point of view, this system also reflects such essential attributes of the Islamic polity as limited separation of powers, supremacy of the leader in all communal affairs and preference for a consultative body rather than the legislative body. Although a form of limited institutional separation of powers is accepted, the constitution (Articles 107-112) grants the *vali-i faqih* a multitude of practically unchecked executive, legislative and judicial responsibilities. Directly and indirectly, through such organs as the Council of Guardians and the Supreme Judicial Council, Khomeini exercised an exceptionally effective control over a broad range of governmental issues including the choice and dismissal of the president and other elected and appointed civilian and military officials and the adoption and implementation of general domestic and foreign policies. The constitutional checks on the *vali-i faqih's* powers are limited and insignificant, and Khomeini chose to ignore such limitation whenever necessary.

Khomeini's charisma—mostly derived from his success in the revolution, his personal attributes, and his simple lifestyle—his ability to skillfully remain outside and above factional disputes and his decisiveness in dealing with the opposition groups—even by violent means if necessary—provided legitimacy for his rule. After Khomeini, however, the legitimacy of the Islamic Republic that is currently a bureaucratic patrimonial system resembling the later *khalifah* system—but with a higher degree of structural differentiation—depends on the leaders' ability to further institutionalize their system and processes and to effectively manage socio-economic and political affairs of the country.

Khomeini's death has made the issue of succession of immediate and vital concern. Although a successor has been chosen, succession will remain the most controversial issue in the practice of *vilayat-i faqih* in the foreseeable future.

NOTES

1. Manzooruddin Ahmed, "Key Political Concepts in the Quran," *Islamic Studies* 10 (June 1971): 88.
2. Cited in Javid Iqbal, "Democracy and the Modern Islamic State," in *Voices of Resurgent Islam*, ed. John L. Esposito (New York: Oxford University Press, 1983), 255.
3. Ruhullah Khomeini, *Nameh-i az Imam-i Mussavi, Kashif al-Ghita* (Tehran: N.p., 1356 A.H.), 27.
4. Ibid.
5. Ali Shariati, *Ummat va Imamate, Ja-al-Haq, The Collection of Speeches* (Tehran: Husayniyyah-i Irshad, 1351 A.H.), 37-38.
6. Ali Shariati, *Tashayyo-i Alavi va Tashayyo-i Safavi* (Tehran: Student Library of the College of Literature and Humanities, 1352 A.H.), 372.
7. Abul A'la Mawdudi, *Islamic Law and Constitution*, trans. Khurshid Ahmad (Lahore: Islamic Publications, 1967), 126.
8. Manzooruddin Ahmed, "The Classical Muslim State," *Islamic Studies* 1 (September 1962): 93.
9. Citations in Taftazani and ibn Human's works are quoted from Ahmed, "The Classical Muslim State," 93.
10. Mawdudi, *Islamic Law and Constitution*, 50, 145.
11. Quoted in Yvonne Y. Haddad, "Sayyid Qutb: Ideologue of Islamic Revival," in *Voices of Resurgent Islam*, ed. John L. Esposito (New York: Oxford University Press, 1983), 77.
12. Mawdudi, *Islamic Law and Constitution*, 178.
13. Quran, 24:55.

14. Quoted in Abul A'la Mawdudi, "Political Theory of Islam," in *Islam in Transition, Muslim Perspectives*, ed. John J. Donohue and John L. Esposito (New York: Oxford University Press, 1982), 258-259.

15. Quran, 4:80.

16. Mawdudi, "Political Theory of Islam," 258.

17. Mawdudi, *Islamic Law and Constitution*, 278.

18. Quoted in Fazlur Rahman, *Islam* (Chicago: University of Chicago Press, 1979), 239.

19. Quran, 4:59.

20. Quoted in Rahman, *Islam*, 239.

21. Iqbal, "Democracy and the Modern Islamic State," 252.

22. Quran, 3:159.

23. Isma'il ibn Umar ibn Kathir, *Tafsir al-Quran al-Azim*, vol. 2 (Cairo: N.p., 1343 A.H.), 277.

24. See Abul Hasan Ali ibn Muhammad al-Mawardi, *Al-Ahkam al-Sultaniyyah*, ed. Maximilian Enger (Bonn: Constitutiones Politicae, 1853), 4; and Abu Muhammad Ali ibn Ahmad ibn Hazm, *Al-Fasl fi'l-Milal wa'l-ahwa'wa'l-nihal*, 5 vols. (Cairo: N.p., 1347-1348 A.H.); and 'Abd al-Rahman ibn Muhammad ibn Khaldun, *Al-Muqaddimah*, ed. E. M. Quatremere (Paris: N.p., 1858), 393-400; and Abu Nasr Muhammad ibn Muhammad ibn Tarkhan al-Farabi, *Kitab fi Mabadi Ara' ahl al-Medinah al-Fadilah*, ed. Fr. Dicterici (Leiden: N.p., 1895), 63.

25. Hamid Behzadi, "The Principles of Legitimacy and Its Influence Upon the Muslim Political Theory," *Islamic Studies* 10 (December 1971): 284.

26. Quoted in Erwin I. J. Rosenthal, "Some Reflections on the Separation of Religion and Politics in Modern Islam," *Islamic Studies* 3 (September 1964): 254.

27. Muhammad Asad, *The Principles of State and Government in Islam* (Berkeley: University of California Press, 1961), 39-40.

28. Sayyid Qutb, *Maarakat al-Islam wa-al-Rasmaliyyah*, 4th ed. (Beirut: Dar al-Shuruq, 1975), 73-74; and Sayyid Qutb, *al-Salaam al-Alami wa-al-Islam* (Beirut: Dar al-Shuruq, 1974), 123.

29. Asad, *The Principles of State*, 42.

30. Charles J. Adams, "Mawdudi and the Islamic State," in *Voices of Resurgent Islam*, ed. John L. Esposito (New York: Oxford University Press, 1983), 123-124.

31. Quoted in Roger M. Savory, "The Problem of Sovereignty in an Ithna 'Ashari ("Twelver") Shi'i State," in *Religion and Politics in the Middle East*, ed. Michael Curtis (Boulder: Westview Press, 1981), 130.

32. Cited in Adams, "Mawdudi and the Islamic State," 115.

33. Iqbal, "Democracy and the Modern Islamic State," 253.

34. Ignaz Goldziher, *Introduction to Islamic Theology and Law*, trans. Andras Hamori and Ruth Hamori (Princeton: Princeton University Press, 1981), 183.

35. Quran, 4:58.

36. Mawdudi, *Islamic Law and Constitution*, 252.

37. Quran, 42:38, 3:159.

38. Cited in Asad, *The Principles of State*, 50.

39. Ahmed, "Key Political Concepts," 93.

40. Asad, *The Principles of State*, 36.

41. Quoted in Godfrey H. Jansen, *Militant Islam* (New York: Harper and Row, 1979), 173.
42. Iqbal, "Democracy and the Modern Islamic State," 256-257.
43. Cited in Adams, "Mawdudi and the Islamic State," 117.
44. Shariati, *Tashayyo-i Alavi va Tashayyo-i Safavi*, 79.
45. George F. Hourani, "The Basis of Authority of Consensus in Sunnite Islam," *Studia Islamica* 21 (1965): 13.
46. Ibid., 44.
47. Ahmad Hasan, "The Argument for the Authority of *Ijma*," *Islamic Studies* 10 (March 1971): 39-40.
48. Asad, *The Principles of State*, 37-38.
49. Cited in Hourani, "The Basis of Authority," 29.
50. Quoted in Hourani, "The Basis of Authority," 44.
51. Asad, *The Principles of State*, 38.
52. Fauzi M. Najjar, "Farabi's Political Philosophy and Shi'ism," *Studia Islamica* 14 (1961): 61.
53. Al-Babu'l-Hadi 'Ashar Hilli, *A Treatise on the Principles of Shi'ite Theology*, trans. William McElwee Miller (London: The Royal Asiatic Society of Great Britain and Ireland, 1928), 66.
54. Shariati, *Ummat va Imamate*, 154, 162, 179, 180.
55. Cited in Rosenthal, "Some Reflections," 263.
56. Muhammad Iqbal, "The Principle of Movement in the Structure of Islam," in *The Reconstruction of Religious Thought in Islam* (Lahore: Kashmiri Bazar, 1968), 174; and John L. Esposito, "Muhammad Iqbal and the Islamic State," in *Voices of Resurgent Islam*, ed. John L. Esposito (New York: Oxford University Press, 1983), 187.
57. Shariati, *Tashayyo-i Alavi va Tashayyo-i Safavi*, 285-286.
58. Iqbal, "Democracy and the Modern Islamic State," 253.
59. For more details see Said Amir Arjomand, "Religion, Political Action and Legitimate Domination in Shi'ite Iran: Fourteenth to Eighteenth Centuries A.D.," *Archives Europeennes De Sociologie* 20 (1979): 59-109.
60. Allamah Sayyid Muhammad Husayn Tabataba'i, *Shi'ite Islam*, trans. and ed. Seyyed Hossein Nasr (Albany: State University of New York Press, 1975), 173.
61. Cited in Michael M. J. Fischer, "Imam Khomeini: Four Levels of Understanding," in *Voices of Resurgent Islam*, ed. John L. Esposito (New York: Oxford University Press, 1983), 164.
62. Shariati, *Ummat va Imamate*, 37.
63. Tabataba'i, *Shi'ite Islam*, 185-186.
64. Seyyed Hossein Nasr, *Ideals and Realities of Islam* (New York: Frederick A. Praeger Publishers, 1967), 160, 162.
65. Moojan Momen, *An Introduction to Shi'i Islam: The History and Doctrines of Twelver Shi'ism* (New Haven: Yale University Press, 1985), 147-148.
66. Quran, 8:33.
67. Quoted in Momen, *An Introduction to Shi'i Islam*, 148.

68. S. Husain M. Jafri, *Origins and Early Development of Shi'a Islam* (London: Longman Group Ltd., 1979), 294.
69. Quran, 4:59.
70. Quran, 33:33.
71. Savory, "The Problem of Sovereignty," 132.
72. Goldziher, *Introduction to Islamic Theology and Law*, 189.
73. Ibid., 188.
74. Shariati, *Tashayyo-i Alavi va Tashayyo-i Safavi*, 161-162, 206, 208.
75. Quran, 33:40.
76. Joseph Elisah, "The Ithna 'Ashari-Shi'i Juristic Theory of Political and Legal Authority," *Studia Islamica* 29 (1969): 23.
77. Shaykh Muhammad ibn Nu'man al-Mufid, *Awa'il al-Maqalat fi'l-Madhab al-Makhtarat* (Tabriz: Ketabfurushi Haqiqat, 1371 A.H.), 12, 39.
78. Elisah, "The Ithna 'Ashari-Shi'i Juristic Theory," 25.
79. Abdulaziz Sachedina, *Islamic Messianism: The Idea of Mahdi in Twelver Shi'ism* (Albany: State University of New York Press, 1981), 1.
80. Quoted in Tabataba'i, *Shi'ite Islam*, 211.
81. For a detailed discussion refer to: W. Montgomery Watt, *The Formative Period of Islamic Thought* (Edinburgh: Edinburgh University Press, 1973).
82. Momen, *An Introduction to Shi'i Islam*, 49.
83. Behzadi, "The Principles of Legitimacy," 284.
84. Goldziher, *Introduction to Islamic Theology and Law*, 220.
85. Sami N. Makarem, "The Philosophical Significance of the Imam in Isma'ilism," *Studia Islamica* 27 (1967): 52.
86. Shariati, *Tashayyo-i Alavi va Tashayyo-i Safavi*, 82-83.
87. Shariati, *Ummat va Imamate*, 44.
88. Ibid., 128, 148, 151, 162-180.
89. Shariati, *Tashayyo-i Alavi va Tashayyo-i Safavi*, 259.
90. Caesar E. Farah, *Islam: Beliefs and Observances* (Woodbury, N.Y.: Baron's Educational Series, 1968), 199.
91. See Najjar, "Farabi's Political Philosophy and Shi'ism," 63, 70-71.
92. See Solomon Pines, "Some Problems of Islamic Philosophy," *Islamic Culture* 11 (1937): 67.
93. See Nikki R. Keddie, "Sayyid Jamal ad-Din 'al-Afghani': A Case of Posthumous Charisma?" in *Philosophers and Kings: Studies in Leadership*, ed. Dankwart A. Rustow (New York: George Braziller, 1970), 158-159.
94. Fauzi M. Najjar, "Democracy in Islamic Political Philosophy," *Studia Islamica* 51 (1980): 119; and Mangol Bayat, "Tradition and Change in Iranian Socio-Religious Thought," in *Modern Iran: The Dialectics of Continuity and Change*, ed. Michael E. Bonine and Nikki R. Keddie (Albany: State University of New York Press, 1981), 48.
95. Quoted in Jansen, *Militant Islam*, 177.
96. Quran, 17:59, 10:63, 2:258, 4:118, 19:48, 3:27, 4:138.
97. Khomeini, *Kashif al-Ghita*, 58, 65.
98. Ruhullah Khomeini, "Islamic Government," in *Islam in Transition, Muslim Perspectives*, ed. John J. Donohue and John L. Esposito (New York: Oxford University Press, 1982), 321.

99. Khomeini, *Kashif al-Ghita*, 60.
100. Ibid., 101-115, 135.
101. Quoted in Khomeini, *Kashif al-Ghita*, 91.
102. Quoted in Ruhullah Khomeini, *Hukumat-i Islami* (Najaf: Nahzat-i Islami Series, 1971), 64, 75.
103. Khomeini, *Hukumat-i Islami*, 70-71, 86, 111-112, and Khomeini, *Kashif al-Ghita*, 95.
104. See Fischer, "Imam Khomeini," 157.
105. Quoted in Haddad, "Sayyid Qutb," 81, and 91.
106. Mawdudi, "Political Theory of Islam," 254.
107. See Adams, "Mawdudi and the Islamic State," 118.
108. A. K. S. Lambton, "A Reconsideration of the Position of the Marja 'al-Taqlid and the Religious Institution," *Studia Islamica* 20 (1964): 124.
109. Ibid., 124-126.
110. See Edward Mortimer, *Faith and Power: The Politics of Islam* (New York: Vintage Books, 1982), 331.
111. Denis M. MacEoin, "The Shi'i Establishment in Modern Iran," in *Islam in the Modern World*, ed. Denis M. MacEoin and Ahmed Al-Shahi (London: Croom Helm, 1983), 94.
112. John Obert Voll, *Islam: Continuity and Change in the Modern World* (Boulder: Westview Press, 1982), 84-86.
113. Shaikh Fadlullah Nuri, "Refutation of the Idea of Constitutionalism," in *Islam in Transition, Muslim Perspectives*, ed. John J. Donohue and John L. Esposito (New York: Oxford University Press, 1982), 293.
114. Ayatullah Murtada Mutahhari, "The Iranian Islamic Movement," in *Islam in Transition, Muslim Perspectives*, ed. John J. Donohue and John L. Esposito (New York: Oxford University Press, 1982), 313.
115. Ruhullah Khomeini, *Balagh, Sokhanan-i Mowsui-i Imam Khomeini* (Tehran: Sepehr Publishing House, 1362 A.H.), 2.
116. Ruhullah Khomeini, *Balagh, Farmayeshat-i Mowsui-i Hazrat-i Imam Khomeini, Rahbar-i Kabir-i Inqilab va Boniangozar-i Jomhoori-i Islami, 1358 A.H.*, vol. 1 (Tehran: Tehran Publishing House, 1361 A.H.), 1:45.
117. Khomeini, *Balagh, Sokhanan-i Mowsui-i Imam Khomeini*, 123.
118. Ali Shariati, *Intizar, Madhab-i Intizar* (Tehran: Husayniyyah-i Irshad Publications, 1350 A.H.), 23-24.
119. Ali Shariati, *Az Kuja Aghaz Kunim* (Tehran: N.p., n.d.), 11.
120. Shariati, *Intizar, Madhab-i Intizar*, 25-29.
121. Khomeini, *Kashif al-Ghita*, 58.
122. Khomeini, *Hukumat-i Islami*, 55, 60-61.
123. Khomeini, *Balagh, Sokhanan-i Mowsui-i Imam Khomeini*, 74-75, 177-178.
124. Khomeini, *Kashif al-Ghita*, 137.
125. Ruhullah Khomeini, *Payamha va Sokhanraniha-ye Imam Khomeini, dar sheshmahe-ye dowom-i sal-i 1359*, vol. 2 (Tehran: Noor Publications, n.d.), 158.
126. Ruhullah Khomeini, *Payamha va Sokhanraniha-ye Imam Khomeini, dar sheshmahe-ye dowom-i sal-i 1360*, vol. 4 (Tehran: Noor Publications, n.d.), 271.
127. Khomeini, *Balagh, Sokhanan-i Mowsui-i Imam Khomeini*, 146.

128. Khomeini, *Kashif al-Ghita*, 63 and 91.
129. Khomeini, *Hukumat-i Islami*, 21, 27, 64.
130. Khomeini, *Kashif al-Ghita*, 98.
131. Khomeini, *Hukumat-i Islami*, 55.
132. Ali Shariati, "Intizar: The Religion of Protest," in *Islam in Transition, Muslim Perspectives*, ed. John J. Donohue and John L. Esposito (New York: Oxford University Press, 1982), 299.
133. Jafri, *Origins and Early Developments of Shi'a Islam*, 47-49, 64-65, 73-76.
134. Tabataba'i, *Shi'ite Islam*, 10.
135. Anwar G. Chejne, *Succession to the Rule in Islam* (Lahore: Kashmiri Bazar, 1960), 22-23, 25.
136. Bryan S. Turner, *Weber and Islam: A Critical Study* (London: Routledge and Kegan Paul, 1974), 85-87.
137. Iqbal, "Democracy and the Modern Islamic State," 255.
138. A. A. A. Fyzee, "Shi'i Legal Theories," in *Origin and Development of Islamic Law*, vol. 1 of *Law in the Middle East*, ed. Majid Khadduri and Herbert J. Liebesny (Washington, D.C.: The Middle East Institute, 1955), 113.
139. Jafri, *Origins and Early Developments of Shi'a Islam*, 281-283.
140. Savory, "The Problem of Sovereignty," 133.
141. Hamid Algar, trans., *Constitution of the Islamic Republic of Iran* (Berkeley: Mizan press, 1980), 29-30.

Conclusion

Many regimes in the Muslim Middle East are currently under pressure by Islamic forces to become Islamic. Some have succumbed to these pressures and have at least nominally committed themselves to Islamic policies, others are resisting these forces with the hope that the growing influence of the revivalist movement—which gained global recognition after its success in the Iranian revolution—is short-lived. However, considering that Islam is an encompassing ideology that covers every aspect of the believer's life, it is unlikely that the ever-significant political role of Islam will disappear or even diminish in Muslim societies. It is generally understood that Islam will play a seminal role in the future developments of the Islamic world, and Islamic forces will continue to demand the ouster of present regimes and their leaders and the installment of Islamic regimes. If these Islamic forces succeed, many of the present regimes will become the victims of legitimacy crises and will eventually be replaced by Islamic systems.

Only history will tell whether the present regimes will be able to withstand the forces of change and whether genuine Islamic systems are attainable in the contemporary conditions of Muslim societies. To even begin to investigate these issues, one has to deal with questions that have haunted Islamic thinkers for centuries. What constitutes an Islamic system? What is the popular role in this system? Who is entitled to rule Muslims societies and what are the leaders' functions? What types of policies should these leaders adopt? With the Muslims' growing hope that the time is right for the establishment of Islamic systems, today these and many more questions are raised and intensely debated among Muslims and observers of Islam.

As a highly regulative ideology, Islam has furnished general and some specific guidelines for the management of all individual and communal affairs. Underscoring the role of authority in the community, Islam has indeed provided instructions regarding the nature and characteristics of the Islamic system. In this system, Muslim thinkers suggest, absolute sovereignty belongs to God alone. The majority, essentially the Sunnis, assert that in view of the direct connection between God and man, immediate sovereignty belongs to man who on behalf of God and in compliance with God's will is responsible for establishing any form of polity that is founded upon and committed to the implementation of Islamic principles. Thus, in this view, the community at large is entitled to manage its affairs as long as it is in compliance with God's will. The Sunni doctrines of delegation and obligation account for a communal role in managing affairs and devise such democratic instruments as *shura*, *ijma* and *bay'ah* to enable the community to make necessary decisions. Shi'i thinkers, classic and contemporary, dismiss the notion of limited popular sovereignty for both theoretical and practical reasons. To them, the community at large is neither entitled nor qualified to manage its affairs. They believe that Muhammad appointed a successor and demanded that authority remain in his family.

Despite this fundamental theoretical/sectarian dispute, Muslims generally agree that the Islamic system is based upon the interrelated Islamic concepts of right/liberty, equality and justice. Compared to democratic-capitalism and socialism, these concepts have distinct meanings in the Islamic world view. In Islam, liberty is essentially defined as total submission to God. Worldly freedoms and rights are presumed to be spurious and unnecessary. While certain socio-economic and political rights are recognized for all individual Muslims and non-Muslim members of the community, in the Islamic system communal rights and needs gain precedence over individual ones. Islamic equality does not entail unmerited socio-economic and political equality of all Muslims. In fact, Islam accepts some degree of inequality. Presumably, this does not make the Islamic path unjust as long as members of the community who are committed to the divinely-ordained ideology and are submissive to God's will are treated equally.

These principles set the Islamic polity apart from both democratic and socialist systems and, in the opinion of many Muslim thinkers, make it a viable and superior alternative to both. The Islamic polity rejects certain aspects of both systems and accepts others. For instance, the Islamic polity dismisses such essential components of democratic-pluralism as the notion of popular sovereignty, pluralism and radical separation of powers and embraces monolithicism and fusion or limited separation of powers that are normally found in socialist systems.

The Islamic economic system also bears significant similarities with socialism and capitalism. Acknowledging individual economic rights, Islam accepts the right of individual believers to private property, as does capitalism, but this right is neither absolute nor is it unlimited. In Islam, absolute ownership belongs to God, and economic demand should be based on need rather than affordability. In pursuit of socio-economic justice and equality, the Islamic system is committed to welfare policies that are common in socialist systems. However, Islam does not intend to establish a classless society nor is it insensitive to the inequalities presently found in all forms of social systems. The Islamic social system accepts the equality of believers regardless of their race and ethno-national origins. Although Islam treats non-believers as second class citizens, it does not presume that such a treatment is unjust.

As in other traditional polities, the lack of a highly institutionalized set of structures and processes accounts for the vital role that leaders play in the Islamic polity. Leaders are an integral part of the polity and thus their functions, legitimacy, and modes of succession to power are essentially determined by the polity. In turn, leaders' attributes and predominantly charismatic roles shape the directions of the system in accordance with God's will. Islamic sectarianism and, to a lesser extent, juridical disputes have been conducive to divergent leadership doctrines. Resorting to the Quranic stipulations, Muhammad's traditions and sayings and pre-Islamic Arab traditional practices, the Sunni majority have taken the position that leadership is a communal affair and as such should be left to the community. Thus, the Sunni doctrine of *khalifah* underscores the role of the community, as the vicegerents of God, in the choice of the caliph. The three interrelated doctrines of *shura, ijma* and *bay'ah* are democratic means designed to facilitate communal input in this matter. Given the fusion or limited separation of powers in the Islamic polity, the caliph's functions are encompassing. He is both the spiritual and temporal authority. As the head of a monolithic and centralized state, the caliph is charged with limited legislative and extensive executive and judicial functions. The caliph's legitimacy depends upon his charismatic and superior human qualities, his leadership skill and success in managing communal affairs and the democratic mode of his succession to power. Of course, this original Sunni doctrine did not remain intact. In response to practical necessities and perhaps under political pressure, Sunni jurists have often modified certain elements of this doctrine.

By relying on the Quran and a series of Islamic sayings and traditions, the Shi'i minority developed a legitimist argument that suggested leadership is a natural right of the prophet and his family. Whereas the Shi'i doctrines of *imamah* were not monolithic, they overwhelmingly dismissed an effective role by the community in the choice of leaders and in the management of communal affairs. Instead, they opted for an appointive process, whereby the ruling imam would formally designate his successor.

Although these original Shi'i thoughts were formulated by Arabs, some even with monarchic proclivities, non-Arab converts to Islam later made enormous contributions to the development of Shi'i thought and the practice of leadership in Shi'ism. For example, the Persian socio-political thoughts and practices were instrumental in the formulation and growth of Safavid Shi'ism that developed an *imamah* doctrine fundamentally different from that of the original—Alid—Shi'ism. Influenced by Persian monarchism and intent on designating the imams a higher status than the caliphs, this revised Shi'ism attached divine qualities to the imams and transformed the appointive process into a system of inheritance, whereby the ruling imam would appoint his eldest son to the leadership of the community. Furthermore, the imams who were originally believed to be both the spiritual and temporal authority gradually lost their political role.

The practice of leadership in Islam does not exactly correspond to these doctrinal positions. In the practice of *khalifah*, the community was neither consulted in the choice of the caliph nor in any other major communal decisions. In practice, the ruling caliph appointed his successor—normally his eldest son—and usually secured communal consent for his choice even by bribery, intimidation and force, if necessary. As the early patriarchal caliphs were gradually replaced by the bureaucratic-patrimonial ones, the caliphs ceased their claim to spiritual authority and simply became political leaders. Various Shi'i factions also followed somewhat similar practices. However, the Shi'i imams never abandoned their claim to temporal authority and, despite periods of quietism during which they solely performed a spiritual function and avoided interference in political affairs, continued to insist that leadership only belongs to the prophet and his progeny.

The nature of the *khalifah* doctrine and the Sunni jurists' receptiveness to major modifications of this doctrine have made the doctrine of *khalifah* more flexible and applicable under different circumstances. The Shi'is, however, have not been able to devise a comprehensive and commonly agreed upon doctrine of leadership for the post-*imamah* era. Some have suggested that, in the absence of the imam, the enlightened and committed Muslims should be in charge of communal affairs. Others, mostly influenced by the Usuli school, insist that the ulama are the most qualified group of believers to govern the community on behalf of the Hidden Imam. This position that is reflected in the doctrine of *vilayat-i faqih* and is being practiced in today's Iran has drawn a tremendous amount of criticism from both Shi'i and Sunni authorities for its doctrinal inaccuracies and practical inadequacies.

The inability of the Islamic Republic to resolve disputes about the scope of governmental authority, the role of the *vali-i faqih*, succession to the rule and policy preferences has added to the continuous debate about the nature of political authority in Islam and its capacity to deal with problems of modern life. Does the true Islamic system maintain the necessary structural and functional features to deal with the complex socio-economic and political issues facing traditional Muslim societies

Conclusion

of the late twentieth century? If not, is it possible to incorporate certain elements of modern systems into the Islamic system in order to make it more applicable to the present day needs of Muslim societies, without sacrificing the basic premises of the Islamic system? To what extent is Islam under pressure to make such adaptations? There are no clear-cut answers to these questions. Recent experiments with the Islamic system in the Arab world, Iran and Pakistan indicate that there is a need for flexibility. It is not clear, however, that the Islamic world is ready to and capable of making such adaptations. Among other things, the success of any system depends upon its ability to deal with its contemporary issues. The Islamic polity and leadership are no exceptions to this rule. Muslims could and should devise systems that are reflective of the spirit of Islam and responsive to today's needs.

Glossary

'adl—social justice.
ahl ar-ra'ay—knowledgeable people.
ajam—non-Arab.
'akhund—an Islamic clergyman usually of low rank.
'alim—(pl. *ulama*) the learned in Islamic jurisprudence.
al-ammah—the public.
amr—(pl. *umur*) "decree," i.e. command of Allah; also a reference to communal affairs.
ansar—"companions" of Muhammad, his followers among the Medinans.
'aql—intellect; the "universal mind" to the Ismailis.
'Ashura—the tenth day of Muharram; the day that Husayn and his companions were massacred by the Umayyad forces.
ayatullah—a high-ranking clergyman.
batini—esoteric, hidden or inner meaning of Allah's word in the Quran.
bay'ah—oath of allegiance.
bida'ah—innovation, heresy, deviation from tradition.
din—term applied to the sum total of a Muslim's faith; religion.
faqih—(pl. *fuqaha*) legal experts; Islamic jurisprudents.
fiqh—Islamic jurisprudence.
ghaybah—occultation of the twelfth imam of Shi'ism.
ghaybat-i kubr—the major occultation of Mahdi.
ghaybat-i suqra—the minor occultation of Mahdi.
Hadith—collection of Muhammad's sayings.
haqqaniyyah—legitimacy of authority.
ijma—consensus of the community and/or learned in the Islamic jurisprudence.
ijtihad—independent judgement on religious matters; a principle of jurisprudence.
'ilm—knowledge.
imamah (imamate)—leadership of the Shi'i imam.
ismah—sinlessness; an attribute of the prophet and imams in Shi'ism.
jahili—ignorant.
jihad—holy war—a war undertaken for the defense and/or expansion of Islam.
ka'far—(pl. *kuffar*) non-believer.
khalifah—the Sunni institution of authority in the post-Muhammad era.
la-din—religionlessness.
ma'ad—resurrection; a reference to the day of return.
Majlis-i barnameh rizi—planning council.
Majlis-i khebregan—council of experts.

Majlis-i shura—consultative body; elected council.
marja-i taqlid—source of emulation; the highest *mujtahid* in Shi'ism whose words and deeds serve as a guide for those unable to exert independent judgement.
ma'sum—infallible and impeccable; a person who is immune from committing sin.
mawla—lord or master; usually a reference to God, the prophet and the early imams.
muhajirin (muhajirun)—emigrants; a reference to those converts who migrated to Medina with Muhammad.
mujtahid—one who exercises *ijtihad* to ascertain a rule of *Shari'ah*; jurisprudent.
al-Nadawa—the pre-Islamic Arab tribal institution that enabled the elders to collectively decide on tribal affairs; assembly.
nahy—prohibition; a reference to the prohibition of Muslims from certain practices.
nass—divine ordinance; specific and formal designation, usually used in relation to the designation of Ali by Muhammad or an imam by his predecessor.
natiq—deputy; the title of individuals who ruled the Twelver community during the minor occultation of Mahdi.
nayib-i imam—imam's deputy; a title used for Khomeini.
niyabah—deputation of the imam.
nubuwwah (nubuwwat)—prophecy.
qadi—(pl. *qudat*) judge who administers the *Shari'ah*.
qadi al-qudat—chief justice.
qayyem—legal guardian.
qiyamah—the day of return.
qiyas—principle of jurisprudence, usually derived by the use of analogical deduction.
rabbaniyyah—supremacy, sovereignty and rule of God.
Ravayah (Ravayat)—imams' sayings.
rawda-kha[w]ni—the act of preaching.
rowshanfikr—(pl. *rowshanfikran*) an enlightened person; an intellectual.
Shari'ah—Islamic legal code.
shumul—comprehensiveness, a reference to the comprehensiveness of the Islamic world view.
shura—consultation; an instrument of democracy in Sunni Islam.
sine zani—a Shi'i ceremonial, usually practiced on the day of *'Ashura*, involving self-flagellation.
Sunnah—corpus of the Traditions.
surah—chapter heading of the Quran.
taqiyyah—dissimulation about one's religious beliefs in order to protect one's self, family, religion and property from harm.
taqlid—emulation, imitation and reliance on precedence or tradition; usually denotes the following of the dictates of one's *mujtahid*.
tawazun—balance, a reference to the balance between the known and the unknown in the Islamic world view.
tawhid—unity; essentially a reference to the unity of God.

Glossary

ta'ziyah—"passion play," staged annually by Shi'is in commemoration of the death of Husayn, the third imam of Shi'ism.

thabat—constancy, a reference to the constancy of the essentials of the Islamic world view.

ummah—Islamic community.

usul ad-din—principal elements of religion (as distinct from *furu ad-din*).

vakil—(pl. *vukala*) also *nayib* (pl. *nuwwab*) deputy.

vilayat-i faqih—leadership of the jurisprudent.

wisayah—the appointive process for the Shi'i imams' succession.

zahiri—exoteric; a reference to the symbolic aspects of religion.

zakat (alms tax)—a religious tax, usually paid to the *marja-i taqlid*, on the believer's net wealth for the purification of his wealth.

zanjir zani—a ceremony practiced by the Twelver Shi'is, usually on the day of *'Ashura*, involving self-flagellation.

zimmis (*dhimmis*)—non-Muslim members of the Islamic community (i.e., Christians and Jews) whose protection is provided for in the Quran.

Bibliography

Arabic and Farsi Sources

al-Farabi, Abu Nasr Muhammad ibn Muhammad ibn Tarkhan. *Kitab fi Mabadi Ara' ahl al-Medinah al-Fadilah.* Edited by Fr. Dicterici. Leiden: N.p., 1895.

ibn Hanbal, Ahmad ibn Muhammad. *Al-Musnad.* Vol. 4. Cairo: Matba'a al-Maymaniyya, 1313 A.H.

ibn Hazm, Abu Muhammad Ali ibn Ahmad. *Al-Fasl fi'l-Milal wa'l-ahwa'wa'l-nihal.* 5 Vols. Cairo: N.p., 1347-1348 A.H.

al-Isfahani, Abu'l-Faraj. *Maqatil al-Talibin.* Najaf: N.p., 1353 A.H.

Kamnimeh Khabarnameh, No. 17. Najaf: National Front of Iran Publications, June 1978.

ibn Kathir, Isma'il ibn Umar. *Tafsir al-Quran al-Azim.* Vol. 2. Cairo: N.p., 1343 A.H.

ibn Khaldun, 'Abd al-Rahman ibn Muhammad. *Al-Muqaddimah.* Edited by E. M. Quatremere. Paris: N.p., 1858.

Khomeini, Ruhullah. *Balagh, Farmayeshat-i Mowsui-i Hazrat-i Imam Khomeini, Rahbar-i Kabir-i Inqilab va Boniangozar-i Jomhoori-i Islami, 1358 A.H.* Vol. 1. Tehran: Tehran Publishing House, 1361 A.H.

———. *Balagh, Sokhanan-i Mowsui-i Imam Khomeini.* Tehran: Sepehr Publishing House, 1362 A.H.

———. *Hukumat-i Islami.* Najaf: Nahzat-i Islami Series, 1971.

———. *Nameh-i az Imam-i Mussavi, Kashif al-Ghita.* Tehran: N.p., 1356 A.H.

———. *Payamha va Sokhanraniha-ye Imam Khomeini,* Vols. 2, 4, and 5. Tehran: Noor Publications, 1361 A.H.

al-Kulayni, Muhammad ibn Ya'qub. *Al-Usul al-Kafi.* Karachi: N.p., 1965.

ibn Maja, Muhammad ibn Yazid. *Sunan.* Vol. 1. Edited by Muhammad Fu'ad 'Abdul Baqi. Cairo: Dar Ihya al-Kutub al-Arabiyya, 1372 A.H.

al-Makki, Ahmad ibn Hajar. *Al-Sawa'iq al-Muhriqa.* Edited by Abdul-Wahhab 'Abdul Latif. Cairo: Maktabat al-Qahira, 1375 A.H.

al-Mawardi, Abul Hasan Ali ibn Muhammad. *Al-Ahkam al-Sultaniyyah.* Edited by Maximilian Enger. Bonn: Constitutiones Politicae, 1853.

al-Mufid, Shaykh Muhammad ibn Nu'man. *Awa'il al-Maqalat fi'l-Madhab al-Makhtarat.* Tabriz: Ketabfurushi Haqiqat, 1371 A.H.

al-Naysaburi, al-Hakim. *Al-Mustadrak.* Vol. 3. Riyad: Maktab al-Nasr al-Haditha, n.d.

Qutb, Sayyid. *Hadha al-Din.* Cairo: Dar al-Qalam, 1962.

———. *Khasais al-Tasawwur al-Islami wa-muqawwamatuhu.* Cairo: Issa al-Babi al-Halabi wa-Shurakauhu, 1962.

———. *Maalim fi al-Tariq.* Cairo: Maktabat Wahbah, 1964.
———. *Maarakat al-Islam wa-al-Rasmaliyyah.* 4th ed. Beirut: Dar al-Shuruq, 1975.
———. *Nahwa Mujtama Islami.* 2d ed. Beirut: Dar al-Shuruq, 1975.
———. *al-Salaam al-Alami wa-al-Islam.* Beirut: Dar al-Shuruq, 1974.
Shariati, Ali. *Az Kuja Aghaz Kunim.* Tehran: N.p., n.d.
———. *Intizar, Madhab-i Intizar.* Tehran: Husayniyyah-i Irshad Publications, 1350 A.H.
———. *Islam Shinasi.* Mashhad: N.p., 1347 A.H.
———. *Tashayyo-i Alavi va Tashayyo-i Safavi.* Tehran: Student Library of the College of Literature and Humanities, 1352 A.H.
———. *Ummat va Imamate, Ja-al-Haq, The Collection of Speeches.* Tehran: Husayniyyah-i Irshad, 1351 A.H.
al-Tabari, Abu Ja'far. *Ta'rikh al-Rusul Wa'l-Muluk.* Vol.1. Edited by M. J. de Goeje. Leiden: E. J. Brill, 1901.
al-Tirmidhi, Abu Isa Muhammad. *Sunan.* Vol. 2. Cairo: Matba'at al-Madani, 1292 A.H.

English and French Sources

Adams, Charles J. "Mawdudi and the Islamic State." In *Voices of Resurgent Islam,* edited by John L. Esposito. New York: Oxford University Press, 1983.
Ahmad, Khurshid. "Islam and the Challenge of Economic Development." In *Islam in Transition, Muslim Perspectives,* edited by John J. Donohue and John L. Esposito. New York: Oxford University Press, 1982.
Ahmed, Manzooruddin. "The Classical Muslim State." *Islamic Studies* 1 (September 1962): 83-104.
———. "Key Political Concepts in the Quran." *Islamic Studies* 10 (June 1971): 77-102.
Algar, Hamid. "Shi'ism and Iran in the Eighteenth Century." In *Studies in the Eighteenth Century Islamic History,* edited by Thomas Naff and Roger Owen. Carbondale: Southern Illinois University Press, 1977.
'Ali, Chiragh. "Islam and Change." In *Islam in Transition, Muslim Perspectives,* edited by John J. Donohue and John L. Esposito. New York: Oxford University Press, 1982.
Aristotle. *The Basic Works of Aristotle.* Edited with an introduction by Richard McKeon. New York: Random House, 1941.
Arjomand, Said Amir. "Religion, Political Action and Legitimate Domination in Shi'ite Iran: Fourteenth to Eighteenth Centuries A.D." *Archives Europeennes De Sociologie* 20 (1979): 59-109.
Aron, Raymond. "Social Structure and the Ruling Class, Part One." *British Journal of Sociology* 1 (1950): 1-16.
Asad, Muhammad. *The Principles of State and Government in Islam.* Berkeley: University of California Press, 1961.
Bachrach, Peter. "Elite Consensus and Democracy." *Journal of Politics* 24 (August 1962): 439-452.

Bibliography

———. *The Theory of Democratic Elitism: A Critique.* Boston: Little, Brown and Co., 1967.
Bacon, Francis. *Selected Writings of Francis Bacon.* Introduction and notes by Hugh G. Dick. New York: Modern Library, 1955.
Bagley, F. R. C. "Religion and the State in Iran." *Islamic Studies* 10 (March 1971): 1-22.
Bani-Sadr, Abul Hasan. "Islamic Economics: Ownership and Tawhid." In *Islam in Transition, Muslim Perspectives,* edited by John J. Donohue and John L. Esposito. New York: Oxford University Press, 1982.
Bayat, Mangol. "Islam in Pahlavi and Post-Pahlavi Iran: A Cultural Revolution?" In *Islam and Development, Religion and Socio-Political Change,* edited by John L. Esposito. New York: Syracuse University Press, 1980.
———. "Tradition and Change in Iranian Socio-Religious Thought." In *Modern Iran: The Dialectics of Continuity and Change,* edited by Michael E. Bonine and Nikki R. Keddie. Albany: State University of New York Press, 1981.
Behzadi, Hamid. "The Principles of Legitimacy and Its Influence Upon the Muslim Political Theory." *Islamic Studies* 10 (December 1971): 277-290.
Bill, James A., and Robert L. Hardgrave, Jr. *Comparative Politics: The Quest for Theory.* Washington, D.C.: The University Press of America, 1981.
Bottomore, T. B. *Elites and Society.* Harmondsworth, Middlesex, England: Penguin Books, 1964.
Brohi, A. K. "The Concept of Islamic Socialism." In *Islam in Transition, Muslim Perspectives,* edited by John J. Donohue and John L. Esposito. New York: Oxford University Press, 1982.
———. *Islam in the Modern World.* 2d ed., edited by Khurshid Ahmad. Lahore: Publisher United Ltd., 1975.
Brunner, Ronald D. "The Policy Sciences as Science." *Discussion Paper No. 4.* Boulder: Center for Public Policy Research, University of Colorado at Boulder, July 8, 1982.
Burns, James MacGregor. *Leadership.* New York: Harper and Row, 1978.
Carr, Edward Hallett. *The New Society.* London: Macmillan and Co., 1960.
Chapra, M. 'Umar. "The Islamic Welfare State." In *Islam in Transition, Muslim Perspectives,* edited by John J. Donohue and John L. Esposito. New York: Oxford University Press, 1982.
Chejne, Anwar G. *Succession to the Rule in Islam.* Lahore: Kashmiri Bazar, 1960.
Clifford-Vaughn, Michalina. "Some French Concepts of Elites." *British Journal of Sociology* 11 (December 1960): 319-331.
Cole, George Douglas Howard. *Studies in Class Structure.* London: Routledge and Kegan Paul, 1955.
Constitution of the Islamic Republic of Iran. Translated by Hamid Algar. Berkeley: 1980.
Cummings, John Thomas, Hossein Askari, and Ahmad Mustafa. "Islam and Modern Economic Change." In *Islam and Development: Religion and Sociopolitical Change,* edited by John L. Esposito. New York: Syracuse University Press, 1980.
Dahl, Robert A. "Critique of the Ruling Elite Model." *American Political Science Review* 52 (June 1958): 463-469.

Dettman, Paul R. "Leaders and Structures in 'Third World' Politics: Contrasting Approaches to Legitimacy." *Comparative Politics* 6 (January 1974): 245-269.
Edinger, Lewis J., ed. *Political Leadership in Industrial Societies: Studies in Comparative Analysis.* New York: John Wiley and Sons, 1967.
_____. "Political Science and Political Biography: Reflections on the Study of Leadership (I)." *Journal of Politics* 26 (May 1964): 423-439.
_____. "Political Science and Political Biography (II): Reflections on the Study of Leadership." *Journal of Politics* 26 (August 1964): 648-676.
Elisah, Joseph. "The Ithna 'Ashari-Shi'i Juristic Theory of Political and Legal Authority." *Studia Islamica* 29 (1969): 17-30.
Esposito, John L. "Introduction: Islam and Muslim Politics." In *Voices of Resurgent Islam*, edited by John L. Esposito. New York: Oxford University Press, 1983.
_____. "Muhammad Iqbal and the Islamic State." In *Voices of Resurgent Islam*, edited by John L. Esposito. New York: Oxford University Press, 1983.
Etzioni, Amitai. *A Comparative Analysis of Complex Organizations: On Power, Involvement, and Their Correlates.* New York: The Free Press, 1961.
Farah, Caesar E. *Islam: Beliefs and Observances.* Woodbury, N.Y.: Baron's Educational Series, 1968.
Faruki, Kemal A. "The Islamic Resurgence: Prospects and Implications." In *Voices of Resurgent Islam*, edited by John L. Esposito. New York: Oxford University Press, 1983.
Field, G. Lowell, and John Higley. *Elitism.* London: Routledge and Kegan Paul, 1980.
Fischer, Michael M. J. "Imam Khomeini: Four Levels of Understanding." In *Voices of Resurgent Islam*, edited by John L. Esposito. New York: Oxford University Press, 1983.
Friedrich, Carl Joachim. *Man and His Government: An Empirical Theory of Politics.* New York: McGraw-Hill, 1963.
_____. *The New Image of the Common Man.* Boston: Beacon Press, 1950. Reprint. Westport, Conn.: Greenwood Press, 1984.
_____. "Political Leadership and Charismatic Power." *Journal of Politics* 23 (February 1961): 14-16.
Froman, Lewis A. Jr. *People and Politics.* Englewood Cliffs: Prentice-Hall, 1962.
Fyzee, A. A. A. "Shi'i Legal Theories." In *Law in the Middle East.* Vol. 1, *Origin and Development of Islamic Law*, edited by Majid Khadduri and Herbert J. Liebesny. Washington, D.C.: The Middle East Institute, 1955.
Gerth, H. H. and C. Wright Mills, eds. *From Max Weber: Essays in Sociology.* Translated with an introduction by H. H. Gerth and C. Wright Mills. New York: Oxford University Press, 1946.
Gerth, H. H. "The Nazi Party: Its Leadership and Composition." *American Journal of Sociology* 45 (January 1940): 517-541.
Giddens, Anthony. "Elites." *New Society* 22 (November 16, 1972): 389-92.
Goldziher, Ignaz. *Introduction to Islamic Theology and Law.* Translated by Andras Hamori and Ruth Hamori. Princeton: Princeton University Press, 1981.
Greenstein, Fred I. "The Impact of Personality on Politics: An Attempt to Clear Away Underbrush." *American Political Science Review* 61 (September 1967): 629-641.

Haddad, Yvonne Y. "Sayyid Qutb: Ideologue of Islamic Revival." In *Voices of Resurgent Islam*, edited by John L. Esposito. New York: Oxford University Press, 1983.

Hasan, Ahmad. "The Argument for the Authority of *Ijma*." *Islamic Studies* 10 (March 1971): 39-52.

―――. "The Political Role of *Ijma*." *Islamic Studies* 8 (June 1969): 135-150.

Hilli, Al-Babu'l-Hadi 'Ashar. *A Treatise on the Principles of Shi'ite Theology*. Translated by William McElwee Miller. London: The Royal Asiatic Society of Great Britain and Ireland, 1928.

Hollander, Edwin P. *Leadership Dynamics: A Practical Guide to Effective Relationships*. New York: The Free Press, 1978.

Holton, Gerald, and Duane H. D. Roller. *Foundations of Modern Physical Science*. Reading, Mass.: Addison-Wesley, 1958.

Hourani, George F. "The Basis of Authority of Consensus in Sunnite Islam." *Studia Islamica* 21 (1965): 13-60.

Iqbal, Javid. "Democracy and the Modern Islamic State." In *Voices of Resurgent Islam*, edited by John L. Esposito. New York: Oxford University Press, 1983.

Iqbal, Muhammad. "Islam as a Moral and Political Ideal." In *Thoughts and Reflections of Iqbal*, edited by Syed Abdul Vahid. Lahore: Ashraf Press, 1964.

―――. "The Principle of Movement in the Structure of Islam." In *The Reconstruction of Religious Thought in Islam*. Lahore: Kashmiri Bazar, 1968.

Ishaque, Khalid M. "The Islamic Approach to Economic Development." In *Voices of Resurgent Islam*, edited by John L. Esposito. New York: Oxford University Press, 1983.

Jafri, S. Husain M. *Origins and Early Development of Shi'a Islam*. London: Longman Group, Ltd., 1979.

Janda, Kenneth F. "Towards the Explication of the Concept of Leadership in Terms of the Concept of Power." In *Political Leadership: Readings for an Emerging Field*, edited by Glenn D. Paige. New York: The Free Press, 1972.

―――. "Towards the Explication of the Concept of Leadership in Terms of the Concept of Power." *Human Relations* 13 (November 13, 1960): 345-363.

Jansen, Godfrey H. *Militant Islam*. New York: Harper and Row, 1979.

Kahin, George M., Guy J. Pauker, and Lucian W. Pye. "Comparative Politics of Non-Western Countries." *American Political Science Review* 49 (December 1955): 1022-41.

Keddie, Nikki R. "Sayyid Jamal ad-Din 'al-Afghani': A Case of Posthumous Charisma?" In *Philosophers and Kings: Studies in Leadership*, edited by Dankwart A. Rustow. New York: George Braziller, 1970.

Keller, Suzanne. *Beyond the Ruling Class: Strategic Elites in Modern Society*. New York: Random House, 1963.

Khomeini, Ruhullah. "Islamic Government." In *Islam in Transition, Muslim Perspectives*, edited by John J. Donohue and John L. Esposito. New York: Oxford University Press, 1982.

Kolabinska, Marie. *La Circulation des Elites en France*. Lausanne: Imprimeries Reunies, 1912.

Lambton, A. K. S. "A Reconsideration of the Position of the Marja 'al-Taqlid and the Religious Institution." *Studia Islamica* 20 (1964): 115-135.

Lasswell, Harold D., Daniel Lerner, and C. Easton Rothwell. *The Comparative Study of Elites: An Introduction and Bibliography*. Stanford: Stanford University Press, 1952.

Lewis, Bernard. "The Return of Islam." In *Religion and Politics in the Middle East*, edited by Michael Curtis. Boulder: Westview Press, 1981.

Loewenstein, Karl. *Max Weber's Political Ideas in the Perspective of Our Time*. Translated by Richard Winston and Clara Winston. Amherst: University of Massachusetts Press, 1966.

MacEoin, Denis M. "The Shi'i Establishment in Modern Iran." In *Islam in the Modern World*, edited by Denis M. MacEoin and Ahmed Al-Shahi. London: Croom Helm, 1983.

al-Mahdi, Al-Sadiq. "Islam—Society and Change." In *Voices of Resurgent Islam*, edited by John L. Esposito. New York: Oxford University Press, 1983.

Mahmud, Mustafa. "Islam vs. Marxism and Capitalism." In *Islam in Transition, Muslim Perspective*, edited by John J. Donohue and John L. Esposito. New York: Oxford University Press, 1982.

Makarem, Sami N. "The Philosophical Significance of the Imam in Isma'ilism." *Studia Islamica* 27 (1967): 41-53.

Mannheim, Karl. *Essays on the Sociology of Culture*. London: Routledge and Paul, 1956.

———. *Ideology and Utopia: An Introduction to the Sociology of Knowledge*. Translated by Louis Wirth and Edward Shils. New York: Harcourt, Brace and Co., 1936.

Marcus, John T. "Transcendence and Charisma." *Western Political Quarterly* 14 (March 1961): 236-241.

Masse, Henri. *Islam*. Translated by Halide Edib. Beirut: Khayats, 1966.

Mawdudi, Abul A'la. *Islamic Law and Constitution*. Translated by Khurshid Ahmad. Lahore: Islamic Publications, 1967.

———. "Political Theory of Islam." In *Islam in Transition, Muslim Perspectives*, edited by John J. Donohue and John L. Esposito. New York: Oxford University Press, 1982.

Meisel, James Hans. *The Myth of the Ruling Class*. Ann Arbor: University of Michigan, 1958.

Michels, Robert. *Political Parties: A Sociological Study of the Oligarchical Tendencies of Modern Democracy*. Translated by Eden Paul and Cedar Paul. New York: The Free Press, 1962.

Minorsky, Vladimir. "Iran: Opposition, Martyrdom, and Revolt." In *Unity and Variety in Muslim Civilization*, edited by Gustave E. Von Grunebaum. Chicago: University of Chicago Press, 1955.

———. "The Rupture Between Sunni and Shi'a in Islam." *Religion* No. 11 (January 1935): 14-20.

Momen, Moojan. *An Introduction to Shi'i Islam: The History and Doctrines of Twelver Shi'ism*. New Haven: Yale University Press, 1985.

Mortimer, Edward. *Faith and Power: The Politics of Islam*. New York: Vintage Books, 1982.

Mosca, Gaetano. *The Ruling Class*. Translated by Hannah D. Kahn. Edited with an introduction by Arthur Livingston. New York: McGraw-Hill, 1939.

Mutahhari, Ayatullah Murtada. "The Iranian Islamic Movement." In *Islam in Transition, Muslim Perspectives*, edited by John J. Donohue and John L. Esposito. New York: Oxford University Press, 1982.

Nadel, S. F. "The Concept of Social Elites." *International Social Science Bulletin* 8 (1956): 413-424.

Na'ini, Shaykh Muhammad Husayn. "Islam and Constitutional Government." In *Islam in Transition, Muslim Perspectives*, edited by John J. Donohue and John L. Esposito. New York: Oxford University Press, 1982.

Najjar, Fauzi M. "Democracy in Islamic Political Philosophy." *Studia Islamica* 51 (1980): 107-122.

―――. "Farabi's Political Philosophy and Shi'ism." *Studia Islamica* 14 (1961): 57-72.

Nasr, Seyyed Hossein. *Ideals and Realities of Islam*. New York: Frederick A. Praeger Publishers, 1967.

―――. *Islam and the Plight of Modern Man*. London: Longman Group, Ltd., 1975.

―――. *Science and Civilization in Islam*. Cambridge, Mass.: Harvard University Press, 1968.

―――. *Three Muslim Sages: Avicenna—Suhrawardi—Ibn 'Arabi*. Cambridge, Mass.: Harvard University Press, 1964.

Nuri, Shaykh Fadlullah. "Refutation of the Idea of Constitutionalism." In *Islam in Transition, Muslim Perspectives*, edited by John J. Donohue and John L. Esposito. New York: Oxford University Press, 1982.

Ogburn, William Fielding. "The Great Man Versus Social Forces." *Social Forces* 5 (December 1926): 225-231.

Paige, Glenn D. *The Scientific Study of Political Leadership*. New York: The Free Press, 1977.

Pareto, Vilfredo. *The Mind and Society*. 4 Vols. Edited by Arthur Livingston. Translated by Andrew Bongiorno and Arthur Livingston. New York: Dover Publications, 1935.

―――. *The Rise and Fall of the Elites: An Application of Theoretical Sociology*. Introduction by Hans L. Zetterberg. Totowa, N.J.: Bedminster Press, 1968.

―――. *Les Systemes Socialistes*. 2 Vols. Paris: Marcel Giard, 1926.

Pfaff, Richard H. "Petrodollars and the Legitimacy Crisis in the Middle East." In *Oil, the Middle East, North Africa and the Industrial States: Developmental and International Dimensions*, edited by Klaus Jurgen Gantzel and Helmut Mejcher. Paderborn, Germany: Ferdinand Schoningh, 1984.

Pines, Solomon. "Some Problems of Islamic Philosophy." *Islamic Culture* 11 (1937): 66-80.

Plamenatz, John and Giovanni Sartori. "Electoral Studies and Democratic Theory." *Political Studies* 6 (February 1958): 1-15.

Quran

Rahman, Fazlur. *Islam*. Chicago: University of Chicago Press, 1979.

―――. "The Islamic Concept of State." In *Islam in Transition, Muslim Perspectives*, edited by John J. Donohue and John L. Esposito. New York: Oxford University Press, 1982.

———. "Some Aspects of Iqbal's Political Thought." *Studies in Islam* 5 (July 1968): 161-166.

Ramazani, R. K. "Shi'ism in the Persian Gulf." In *Shi'ism and Social Protest*, edited by Juan R. I. Cole and Nikki R. Keddie. New Haven: Yale University Press, 1986.

Ratnam, K. J. "Charisma and Political Leadership." *Political Studies* 12 (1964): 341-354.

al-Raziq, Ali 'Abd. "The Caliphate and the Basis of Power." In *Islam in Transition, Muslim Perspectives*, edited by John J. Donohue and John L. Esposito. New York: Oxford University Press, 1982.

Rose, Gregory. "Velayat-e-Faqih and the Recovery of Islamic Identity in the Thought of Ayatollah Khomeini." In *Religion and Politics in Iran: Shi'ism from Quietism to Revolution*, edited by Nikki R. Keddie. New Haven: Yale University Press, 1983.

Rosenthal, Erwin I. J. "The Role of the State in Islam: Theory and the Medieval Practice." Paper presented to the Colloquium on Tradition and Change in the Middle East, Harvard, 1968.

———. "Some Reflections on the Separation of Religion and Politics in Modern Islam." *Islamic Studies* 3 (September 1964): 249-284.

Rustow, Dankwart A. "Introduction to the Issue Philosophers and Kings: Studies in Leadership." *Daedalus* 97 (Summer 1968): 683-694.

———. *A World of Nations: Problems of Political Modernization*. Washington, D.C.: Brookings Institution, 1967.

Sachedina, Abdulaziz. "Ali Shariati: Ideologue of the Iranian Revolution." In *Voices of Resurgent Islam*, edited by John L. Esposito. New York: Oxford University Press, 1983.

———. *Islamic Messianism: The Idea of the Mahdi in Twelver Shi'ism*. Albany: State University of New York Press, 1981.

Sanhoury, A. *Le Califat*. Paris: Geuthner, 1926.

San Juan, E., Jr. "Orientations of Max Weber's Concept of Charisma." *The Centennial Review* 11 (Spring 1967): 270-285.

Sartori, Giovanni. "Concept Misformation in Comparative Politics." *American Political Science Review* 64 (December 1970): 1033-1053.

Savory, Roger M. "The Problem of Sovereignty in an Ithna 'Ashari ("Twelver") Shi'i State." In *Religion and Politics in the Middle East*, edited by Michael Curtis. Boulder: Westview Press, 1981.

Schumpeter, Joseph A. *Capitalism, Socialism and Democracy*. 3d ed. New York: Harper and Bros., 1950.

———. *Imperialism and Social Classes*. Translated by Heinz Norden. Edited with an introduction by Paul M. Sweezy. New York: Augustus M. Kelley, Inc., 1951.

Searing, Donald D. "Models and Images of Man and Society in Leadership Theory." In *Political Leadership: Readings for an Emerging Field*, edited by Glenn D. Paige. New York: The Free Press, 1972.

Seligman, Lester G. "The Study of Political Leadership." *American Political Science Review* 44 (December 1950): 904-915.

Sereno, Renzo. "The Anti-Aristotelianism of Gaetano Mosca and Its Fate." *Ethics* 48 (1937-1938): 509-518.
Shaltut, Shaykh Mahmud. "Socialism and Islam." In *Islam in Transition, Muslim Perspectives*, edited by John J. Donohue and John L. Esposito. New York: Oxford University Press, 1982.
Shariati, Ali. "Intizar: The Religion of Protest." In *Islam in Transition, Muslim Perspectives*, edited by John J. Donohue and John L. Esposito. New York: Oxford University Press, 1982.
Shils, Edward. "The Concentration and Dispersion of Charisma: Their Bearing on Economic Policy in Underdeveloped Countries." *World Politics* 11 (October 1958-July 1959): 1-19.
Tabataba'i, Allamah Sayyid Muhammad Husayn. *Shi'ite Islam*. Translated and edited with an introduction and notes by Seyyed Hossein Nasr. Albany: State University of New York Press, 1975.
Taliqani, Ayatullah Mahmud. "The Characteristics of Islamic Economics." In *Islam in Transition, Muslim Perspectives*, edited by John J. Donohue and John L. Esposito. New York: Oxford University Press, 1982.
Tucker, Robert C. *Politics as Leadership*. Columbia: University of Missouri Press, 1981.
──────. "The Theory of Charismatic Leadership." *Daedalus* 97 (Summer 1968): 731-758.
al-Turabi, Hassan. "The Islamic State." In *Voices of Resurgent Islam*, edited by John L. Esposito. New York: Oxford University Press, 1983.
Turner, Bryan S. *Weber and Islam: A Critical Study*. London: Routledge and Kegan Paul, 1974.
Voll, John Obert. *Islam: Continuity and Change in the Modern World*. Boulder: Westview Press, 1982.
Von Grunebaum, Gustave E. *Islam: Essays in the Nature and Growth of a Cultural Tradition*. New York: Barnes and Noble, 1961.
Watt, W. Montgomery. *The Formative Period of Islamic Thought*. Edinburgh: Edinburgh University Press, 1973.
──────. "Shi'ism Under the Umayyads." *Journal of the Royal Asiatic Society of Great Britain and Ireland* Parts 3 and 4 (1960): 158-172.
──────. "The Significance of the Early Stages of Imami Shi'ism." In *Religion and Politics in Iran: Shi'ism from Quietism to Revolution*, edited by Nikki R. Keddie. New Haven and London: Yale University Press, 1983.
Weber, Max. *The Theory of Social and Economic Organization*. Translated by A. M. Henderson and Talcott Parsons. New York: Oxford University Press, 1947.
Wolff, Kurt H., ed. *The Sociology of George Simmel*. New York: Free Press of Glencoe, 1950.

Index

Abbas (Shah), 69
Abbasids, 114, 115
Abidin, Ali Zayn al-, 70, 116
Abu-Bakr, 62, 63, 113, 115
Abu-Muslim, 67, 71
Afghani, Jamal ad-Din al-, 104
Agriculture, 16
Ahmed, Manzooruddin, 38–39, 75
Ahsa'i, Shaikh Ahmad, 104
Akhbaris, 108
Ali, 62, 63, 64, 65, 71, 77, 91, 100, 113
'Ali, Chiragh, 37
Ali, Zayd ibn, 98
Allah. *See* God
Allah, Ubayd, 99
'Amili, Shaykh Muhammad al-Hurr al-, 67
Appointment, doctrine of, 102
Arabs, 65–66, 68–69, 71, 82, 88–89, 114
Aristotle, 11, 14, 67
Aron, Raymond, 23
Asad, Muhammad, 40, 82, 89
Ascriptiveness, 19, 29

Bachrach, Peter, 23
Bacon, Francis, 21
Bani-Sadr, Abul Hasan, 50
Baqir, Muhammad al-, 94, 117
Bay'ah, 83, 91, 113, 128, 129
Behavioralism, 6
Bottomore, T. B., 23–24
Brohi, A. K., 49, 51–52
Burns, James MacGregor, 7, 10

Caliphs, 4, 81–84. *See also Khalifah*; Leadership; Rightly-Guided Caliphs
Capitalism, 42, 50, 51–52, 128
Charisma
  concept of, 24–26
  functionalist theories, 26–27
  and Islamic leadership, 28–30, 112
  and legitimacy of authority, 27–28
  and social movements, 27
  theories of charismatic authority, 2, 24–30
Christianity, 69, 97, 98
Classes, 14–15, 16, 22
Cole, George D. H., 13
Communal consent, doctrine of. *See Ijma*
Communism, 42, 55
Consensus, doctrine of. *See Ijma*
Consultation, doctrine of. *See Shura*
Council of Guardians, 119

Dahl, Robert, 24
Delegation, doctrine of, 78–80, 128
Democracy, 128
  and elitism, 22–24
  and *ijma*, 90
  and Islamic state, 40–42, 45, 54–55, 87
  and *khalifah*, 80
  and stratification, 16
de Rousiers, P., 14
Despotism, 18
Determinism, 11, 21–22, 29
Divine Law, 79, 80, 82, 99

Edinger, Lewis, 6, 9

Elite(s)
  circulation, 20–21, 24
  and classless society, 22
  concept of, 13–14
  decline of, 21
  definitions, 13
  in democracies, 16, 17. *See also* Elite theories, and democratic thought
  in developed societies, 18
  emergence and proliferation, 15–16
  functions, 18–19
  and human nature, 15
  and *ijma*, 42
  intra-elite relationship, 11, 20–21
  Islamic, 29
  and *al-Nadawa*, 86
  nineteenth century, 22
  plurality, 14, 23
  polarization, 29
  recruitment, 19, 29
  strategic, 13
  sub-elites, 15
  See also Elite theories
Elite theories, 2, 12–24
  coercion vs. persuasion, 17
  cohesion and polarity, 16–17
  and democratic thought, 22–24. *See also* Elite(s), in democracies
  elite-follower relationship, 11, 17–18
  evaluation of, 24
  and Islamic leadership, 28–30
  and Marxism, 21–22
  philosophical foundations, 103–104
  psychological factors in, 20, 21
  and social stratification, 13, 16, 22
  vilayat-i faqih, 104–106. *See also* Vilayat-i faqih
  See also Elite(s)
Etzioni, Amitai, 13

Farabi, Abu Nasr al-, 40, 90, 103, 104
Faruki, Kemal A., 89
Fascism, 23, 55
Fassi, Allal al-, 104

Fatimah, 72, 116
Ferdowsi, Abul Qasim, 67
Field, G. Lowell, 17
Friedrich, Carl, 13, 16, 25

Ghadir Khum, 62, 63
Ghazali, Muhammad al-, 36, 76, 88
Gnosticism, 67
God, 4, 41, 43–44, 45, 78–79, 127–128
Goldziher, Ignaz, 68, 84, 95
Great-man theory, 77

Hadith, 45, 63, 80, 86, 89, 97, 98
Hanafiyyah, Muhammad ibn, 117
Hanbal, Ahmad ibn, 63, 86
Hasan, 116
Hegel, 11
Hermeticism, 67
Hidden Imam. *See* Mahdi
Higley, John, 17
Hollander, Edwin, 8, 9
Husayn, 68, 70, 71, 116, 117

Ibn Babuyah, 66
Ibn Human, 78
Ibn-Rushd, 40
Ideologism, 12
Ijma, 40–41, 45, 62, 88–91, 111, 128, 129
Ijtihad, 90
Imamah, 4, 29, 38, 62, 64, 69, 70, 71–72, 76, 78, 92–102, 115–117
Iqbal, Muhammad, 41
Iran, 3, 29, 50, 69, 70, 102, 107–108, 112, 118–120, 130
Isfahan, 67
Ishraqis, 67
Islam(ic), 127, 128
  belief system, 1, 35
  current revivalist movement, 38
  and democracy. *See* Democracy
  development of, 67
  elites, 29
  expansion of, 66
  legal code. *See* Shari'ah

Index

monolithicism. *See* Monolithicism and politics, 35–38
polity, 2, 3
and power, 35, 46
state. *See* Islamic state
universality of, 35, 37, 39
vicegerency of man, 43, 45
Islamic Republic of Iran. *See* Iran
Islamic state
  authority of, 54–55
  branches of, 46–49
  characteristics of, 44–56
  consultative council, 47–49
  divine origin, 43–44
  earnings in, 50–51
  economic system, 49–52, 128
  equality in, 41, 52–53, 128, 129
  factionalism in, 44
  foreign policies, 55
  foundations of, 38–39
  fusion of powers, 46
  individual vs. communal rights in, 50
  judiciary in, 49, 84, 115
  leadership in, 47. *See also* Leadership
  legislative function in, 47, 84, 115
  liberty in, 41
  monolithicism of, 44, 46. *See also* Monolithicism
  non-Muslims in, 53, 129
  political system, 44–49
  private property in, 50, 128
  social system, 52–54
  taxation in, 51
  uniqueness of, 40–44
  See also Islam(ic)
Ismah, 95
Ismailis, 67, 72, 99–100

Janda, Kenneth, 8–9
Jaza'iri, Sayyid Murtada, 107
Jihad, 55, 84
Justice, 49, 55

Kazim, Musa al-, 106

Keller, Suzanne, 13, 16, 17, 19
Khalifah, 4, 29, 38, 64, 65, 69, 70, 71, 78–91, 112–115, 129, 130
Khattab, Umar ibn, 63
Khomeini, Ruhullah
  and equality, 53
  and Islamic state, 39, 41, 46, 49
  and leadership, 36, 76, 92, 110
  and political activity, 36
  and ulama, 108–109, 111
  and *vilayat-i faqih*, 92, 105–106, 107, 110–112, 119–120
  and violence, 56
Kirchenrecht (Sohm), 25
Koran. *See* Quran

Lasswell, Harold, 13, 14
Leadership
  definitions, 7–8
  functions of, 83–84, 110–111
  hereditary succession of, 113–114, 116
  indispensability of, 76–77
  Islamic, 29–30
  legitimacy of, 81–83, 110, 114
  operationalization of concept, 9
  and *politics* (term), 8
  post-*Imamah*, 118–120
  and power, 7–8
  pragmatism in, 112–120
  qualities of leaders, 11, 28, 81–82, 100, 109–110. *See also* Charisma
  relational nature of, 7, 29
  revolutionary vs. reformist, 18–19
  and societal needs, 36
  study of, 5–6, 9–10
  and succession, 4, 19, 63–64, 66, 101–102
  temporal vs. religious, 117
  See also Leadership, theories of
Leadership, theories of
  behavioralism, 6
  charismatic authority. *See* Charisma, theories of charismatic authority
  contemporary doctrines, 103–112

and determinism, 11. *See also*
　Determinism
elite. *See* Elite theories
historicism, 11
mechanistic models, 10–11, 12
Multivariate, Multidimensional
　Linkage approach, 9
organismic models, 11, 12
and scientific method, 10
Transactional approach, 9
See also Leadership
Lewis, Bernard, 35–36
Loewenstein, Karl, 25

Mahdi, 4, 41, 72, 77, 92, 97, 117–118
Mahmud, Mustfa, 51
Maja, Muhammad ibn Yazid ibn, 86
Majlisi, Muhammad Baqir, 67
Makarem, Sami N., 99
Mannheim, Karl, 14, 16, 23
Marx, Karl, 11, 20. *See also* Marxism
Marxism, 20, 21–22. *See also* Marx,
　Karl
Materialism, 42, 51, 52
Mawdudi, Abul A'la, 37, 39, 45, 47–48, 52–53, 53–54, 55, 77, 78–79, 80, 83, 84, 88, 106–107
Mazda, 66
Meritocracy, 19, 29
Messianism, 97–98
Methodology, 8–10
Michels, Robert, 15–16, 21
Mills, C. Wright, 15, 16
Minorsky, Vladimir, 70
Monarchism, 65–66, 67, 69, 70, 87, 102, 112, 119
Monolithicism, 44, 46, 61–64, 128
Monotheism, 35, 36, 43
Morality, 37
Mosca, Gaetano, 11, 14–15, 20, 22
Mu'awiyyah, 114, 116
Muhammad (Prophet), 44, 49, 56, 80–81, 99, 112
　Medinan period, 64
　succession to, 4, 61, 63–64, 77, 106
　See also Hadith; Sunnah
Mukarrib, 66

Musayyarah (ibn Human), 78
Mutahhari, Murtada, 108

Nadawa, al-, 63, 65, 86
Na'ini, Shaykh Muhammad Husayn, 53
Nasr, Seyyed Hossein, 62
Natural right, doctrine of, 30, 102
Nawbakhti, Abul Qasim Husayn ibn Ruh, 118
Neo-Platonism, 67, 99, 103–104. *See also* Plato
Neo-Pythagoreanism, 67
Nuri, Shaikh Fadlullah, 108

Obligation, doctrine of, 78, 80–81
Occultation, doctrine of, 97, 98, 117
Ogburn, William, 11
Ottoman empire, 69, 70

Pahlavis, 119
Paige, Glenn, 5, 9
Pakistan, 3
Pareto, Vilfredo, 11, 13, 14, 15, 16–17, 20, 21, 22
Patrimonialism, 4, 46, 75, 113
Persians, 66–67, 68–69, 70–71, 129–130
Pfaff, Richard, 27
Plato, 8, 11, 14, 18. *See also* Neo-Platonism
Popular sovereignty. *See* Democracy
Prophecy, 79, 99

Qaddafi, Muammar, 36
Qajar dynasty, 119
Quietism, 4, 68, 72, 98
Quran, 36, 37, 38, 43, 44, 45, 49, 79, 82
　and contractual commitments, 56, 91
　and individual responsibilities, 50–51
　and justice, 55
　and non-Muslims, 68
　and obligation, 80–81

Index

and succession to Muhammad, 62–63
Quraysh family, 82, 95, 100, 101
Qutb, Sayyid, 37, 42–43, 50, 52, 55, 79, 82, 106

Raziq, Ali 'Abd al-, 37–38
Reciprocity. *See* Elite theories, elite-follower relationship
Republic (Plato), 11
Rida, Muhammad Rashid, 81–82, 90
Rightly-Guided Caliphs, 45, 47, 63, 84, 112–113, 115
Rowshanfikran, 111–112
Rustow, Dankwart, 9

Saba, 'Abdallah ibn, 65
Sadiq, Ja'far as-, 94–95, 106, 117
Safavids, 39, 66, 69, 70, 96, 118
Saint-Simon, 13, 14
Sartori, Giovanni, 6
Sasanids, 69, 70
Satanic politics, 36
Savory, Roger M., 70
Schumpeter, Joseph A., 20, 22, 23
Searing, Donald, 10, 11
Sectarianism, 3, 61–62
Secularism, 35, 36, 37, 38
Seligman, Lester, 7, 9, 30–31(n12)
Sereno, Renzo, 15
Seveners. *See* Ismailis
Shafii, al-, 48
Shahid, Zayd al-, 72
Shahnameh (Ferdowsi), 67
Shahr al-Maqasid (Taftazani), 78
Shahrbanu, 70
Shaikhis, 104, 108
Shaltut, Shaykh Mahmud, 37
Shaoobi movement, 69
Shari'ah, 37, 39, 40, 44, 45, 46, 47, 82–83, 86
  interpretation of, 48
  sources of, 97
  three principles of, 49, 52
Shariati, Ali, 35, 36, 39, 41, 69, 71, 76, 88, 90, 93, 96, 102, 109, 111–112

Shariatmadari, Muhammad Kadem, 93, 107
Shaykhu't-Ta'ifa, 66
Shi'ism, 4, 29, 30, 41–42, 45
  Alid, 39, 71, 130
  clerics in Iran, 107–108
  development of, 67
  and disunity, 62–63
  factions in, 68, 70, 71–72, 96–97
  and *ijma*, 89–90
  and *ijtihad*, 90
  and *imamah*, 92–102
  Imami. *See* Shi'ism, Ithna 'Ashari
  imams' functions in, 63, 84
  Ismailiyyah, 99–100
  Ithna 'Ashari, 72, 76, 93, 94, 95, 96, 97–98, 116–117. *See also* Twelvers
  and leadership, 76–77, 130
  and non-Muslims, 68
  and Persian thought, 66–67
  Safavid, 39, 71, 90, 95, 96, 130
  and *shura*, 85–86
  and succession, 64, 65. *See also* Imamah
  –Sunnism division, 62, 65, 68, 115–116
  and *taqiyyah*, 96
  Zaydiyyah, 88, 98–99, 119
Shura, 41–42, 45, 47, 62, 83, 85–88, 89, 128
Simmari, Ali ibn Muhammad, 118
Socialism, 42, 51–52
Social stratification, 13, 16, 22, 29
Sohm, Rudolph, 25
South Arabia, 66
Spencer, Herbert, 11
Sufism, 66, 67, 94
Suhrawardi, Shihab ad-Din, 67
Sunnah, 37, 44–45, 47, 63
Sunnism, 4, 29, 37, 47, 48, 78–91, 127–128
  and Arabism, 71
  and *ijma*, 88–89
  and *imamah*, 92–93
  and Muhammad, 95–96

and non-Muslims, 68
and Persians, 71
–Shi'ism division, 62, 65, 68, 115–116
and *shura*, 85–86
and succession, 62–63, 64, 83, 85. *See also Khalifah*
Supreme Judicial Council, 119

Tabataba'i, Muhammad Husayn, 93
Taftazani, Sa'd ad-Did, 78
Taliqani, Mahmud, 50, 107
Tamiyyah, Ahmad ibn, 80
Taqiyyah, 96
Taqlid, 90
Tawhid, 35, 61
Taxation, 51
Theodoros (King), 98
Third World, 5
Totalitarianism, 54–55
Treason, 46
Tucker, Robert, 8
Twelvers, 4, 67, 68, 70, 72, 102. *See also* Shi'ism, *Ithna 'Ashari*

Ulama, 67, 89, 90, 92, 108–109, 130
Umar, 113
Umari, Muhammad ibn Uthman, 118
Umari, Uthman ibn Sa'id, 118
Ummah, 115
Umayyads, 114, 115, 116
Usulis, 108, 119
Usury, 51
Uthman, 113

Vilayat-i faqih, 92, 104–106, 107, 109–112, 119–120, 130
Violence, 55, 56
Virtuous City, 104

Watt, W. Montgomery, 72
Weber, Max, 24–25, 25–26, 28, 93
Welfare-statism, 12

Yazdigird III, 70
Yazid, 114, 116

Zakat, 51
Zaydis, 72, 88. *See also* Shi'ism, *Zaydiyyah*
Zoroastrianism, 66, 67, 68, 97